Worth doing Twice

krause publications

700 East State Street, Iola, WI 54990-0001
www.krause.com

Please call or write for our free catalog of publications. Our toll-free number to place an order or obtain a free catalog is 800-258-0929 or please use our regular business telephone 715-445-2214 for editorial comment and further information.

The following registered trademark terms and companies appear in this publication:
"Harrison Rose" ©1930
Orvus Paste®
Safeguard®
Olfa® Cutter
Berol© Karismacolor
Berol© Prismacolor
Berol© Verithin
Chakoner®
Gingher®
Magic Sizing®
Band-Aid®
Plexiglas®
Cotton Classic®
Soft Touch®
Cotton Choice®
Quilt Lite®
Thermore®
"Cute Little Designs for the Children"©

Illustrations by Lori Hale
Book design by Jan Wojtech
Photo Credits:
All before photography by Jeannette T. Muir
All completed quilt photography by James W. Muir, except those on pages 19, 21, 23, 27, 37, 41, 46, and 53, by John W. Gallinelli

Library of Congress Cataloging-In-Publication Data

Morris, Patricia J. and Jeannette T. Muir
    Worth doing twice
        1. quilting   2. quilt history   3. title

ISBN 0-87341-706-2
CIP 98-87382

FOR

Bill, Jim, Julie, Kathy, and Helen

ACKNOWLEDGMENTS

Thanks: To our husbands for their encouragement, support, and help; To Kay Lukasko for her keen eye, clear head, and efficiency; To the unknown quiltmakers of yesterday who constructed the tops we so enjoy completing; To Meredith Schroeder at AQS for permission to use material published in *Precision PATCHWORK for Scrap Quilts Anytime, Anywhere*; To the staff at Krause Publications for smoothing the way to publication.

TABLE OF CONTENTS

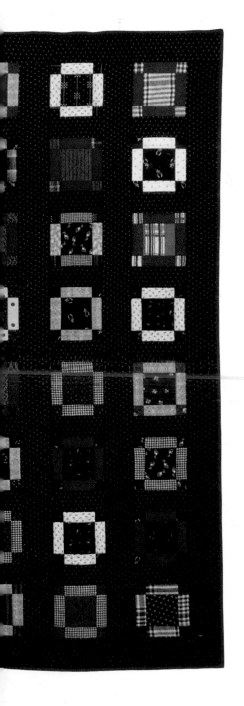

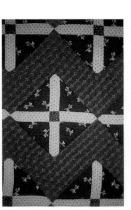

Chapter 9: Quilt Projects: Making Your Own "Heirloom" 65

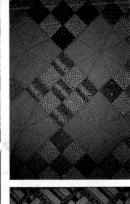

INTRODUCTION

Remember those years when you were growing up? For most of us, whenever we were content with completing something in a less than acceptable manner, our mothers, grandmothers, and aunts told us that, "A thing worth doing is worth doing well." In this book, Jeannette and Pat put a somewhat different spin on this adage and apply it to quilts: "A thing worth doing is worth doing twice."

The purpose of *Worth Doing Twice* is to cover the renovation, reconstruction, and reproduction of old quilt tops dating from the 1870s to the 1950s. The thrust of these activities is to save old quilt tops from certain extinction and/or to make your own "heirloom" quilt.

Worth Doing Twice focuses on an informative, practical, and light-hearted approach that avoids the "thou shalt not touch" attitude of some diehard conservatives. Mind, of course, we are not talking here about museum-quality quilt tops, but rather of reconstructing the orphans of the quilt world. These are often not well-made and would be doomed to being boxed and stored in an attic or basement (or, heaven forbid, cut up for dust rags, toys, or clothing) if not rescued and lovingly finished. We feel that completing these works is a way of respecting the original maker's plans (and even hopes and dreams), as well as creating an enjoyable activity for today's quiltmakers. Whether the work was begun by a "blood relative" or a "quilt relative," the twice finished piece can only bring pleasure.

The genesis of *Worth Doing Twice* was a quilt show in Knoxville, Tennessee, in June of 1990. While helping friends set up their vendor space, Jeannette was "attacked" by an outrageously ugly quilt top. Technically, the top was a horror with no seams matching, the plain blocks not the same size as the pieced blocks, and, to top it off, every color of fabric imaginable was used.

Yet, Jeannette surrendered to the lure of the top. At another time on that same day, and in the same vendor's booth, unbeknownst to Jeannette, Pat was "captured" by two old tops. Not to be outdone, the following day Jeannette returned to the same vendor and got a second "needs a little love" quilt top for herself.

This was the start, for both Jeannette and Pat, of what has become a passion: to seek out unusual, funky-looking, and inexpensive tops. As a friend puts it, "tops that make your heart sing," even if sometimes these tops make you laugh out loud. But for whatever reason, there is a tremendous satisfaction in completing the work of an earlier quiltmaker (or duplicating it). So Pat and Jeannette both continue to fall victim to the siren song of these strangely wonderful quilt tops.

Generally speaking, these odd-ball quilt tops need some degree of repair before they can be sandwiched and quilted. This task can require hunting down vintage or reproduction fabrics in some cases or, in others, picking the whole top apart (a "picker") and resewing it. In this book you will find photos of the quilt tops as purchased and as completed, as well as patterns for some of the tops, plus directions for reproducing them. The quilt top designs that appear in this book are either old enough that they are in the public domain or they are included here by permission.

Enjoying this form of our quilt heritage, we hope to interest others in this same pursuit. It will save some tops for posterity while affording us the pleasure of doing the work. Keep your eyes open for any old "tops that make your heart sing" or put a grin on your face.

CHAPTER 1

WHY COMPLETE OLD TOPS?

Because we are usually very busy people, we are questioned about why we are working on completing old tops. Family, friends, colleagues, and total strangers are curious why we spend our time in this way and few hesitate to ask us about it.

As with so many other things, we have no single reason for our activity; there are any number of reasons for doing this. Sometimes an old quilt top has "X" reason for completing it, while another old quilt top has "Y" for finishing, and yet another top may have both "X" and "Y" reasons for working on it. But one way or the other, we do have our reasons!

Many people have a passion for collecting old quilts, but because these are steadily going up in price, such a collection can be prohibitively expensive. Old quilt tops are far less expensive and, even though they may require some work to prepare for finishing, plus quilting, binding, attaching a sleeve, and a label, they can be the basis for a good quilt collection.

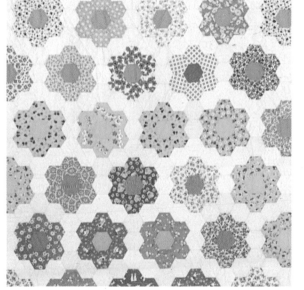

Some quilters simply find a good deal of satisfaction in completing the old tops and saving them from oblivion. It is also a way of connecting with our quilt heritage and can be a very therapeutic activity.

This restoration and completion of old tops not only saves these works from oblivion but also saves them from becoming "cutter" quilts and ending up as teddy bears or vests. Of course, if you come across a museum-quality top, you'd want to be very careful about how you finish it or you might even ask if you should finish it. Fine museum-quality tops can be recognized by their condition, fine workmanship, use of good fabrics, and integrated design. Judgments about whether or not to finish any given quilt top have to be made on an individual basis.

Generally, the affordable tops available range from the 1870s to the 1950s. Those that stem from after the big new interest in quilting, the 1970s forward, do not seem as appealing as the earlier tops and a great number of them are made with blends which many quiltmakers do not find as aesthetically pleasing as all-cotton tops. Also, many of the tops from this later period were, and are, being made as learning samplers in basic quiltmaking courses and as such have a sameness to them; they are probably not worth finishing now (but maybe in a hundred years!).

Old quilt tops provide an excellent inspiration for making reproductions. These old tops can be a guideline for making copies, using reproduction fabrics or the exciting new fabrics of today.

Still, in our estimation, the best reason for finishing old tops is the pleasure and therapy derived from working on them and the delight in seeing a piece completed, with the resultant extended life.

CHAPTER 2

SOURCES FOR OLD TOPS

Once you decide it might be rewarding and fun to try your hand at restoring and completing an old top, the obvious first step is obtaining one to work on. You may be fortunate enough to own some old family quilt tops which you can use. But, unfortunately, most of us don't have these and have to look elsewhere.

Start searching close to home by checking with other family members and friends. When they hear that you want to give new life to a quilt top, they may be willing to give them to you or sell them to you at a reasonable price.

Reaching a little farther from home, check out all of the yard sales, garage sales, auctions, estate sales, resale shops, and antique shops in your area. It seems that the further out from a major city that you hunt the better luck you will have in finding old quilt tops—sometimes yard sales in small towns beyond suburbia can be treasure troves for quilt tops. Some treasures have even been found in car trunks and trash cans. Antique shops that carry a broad spectrum of goods are a reasonable place to look for tops, although, generally speaking, the tops can be pricey at these shops.

Quilt and quilt top vendors at major quilt shows (as well as some smaller shows) are excellent sources. They usually have quite a few tops for sale, ranging in ages, patterns, sizes, colors, fabrics, and prices. Some vendors are willing to discuss price, and you may be able to save a few dollars this way. Most of the vendors also carry old blocks, some in sets and some individual ones. You may choose to buy blocks to make into a quilt instead of starting with an entire top.

By far the majority of quilt tops we have completed, are working on, or that are awaiting our attention have been purchased from quilt show vendors. Purchasing quilt tops saves you the trouble of hunting them down yourself, spending inordinate amounts of time looking for them, plowing through all kinds of other things to locate them, and being knowledgeable about values, etc. We are willing to pay extra for the vendors to do the searching step. See the Resource List for reliable sources.

When you see a quilt top that needs work and it appeals to you, your next consideration should be your budget. Give some thought beforehand about what is the highest price you are willing to pay. It's much too easy to get carried away, and you may spend too much unless you have this figure in the back of your mind as a guideline.

Prices for old tops can vary greatly depending on many factors, such as age, condition, size, and so forth. The one factor that seems to govern the prices most is where it is purchased. This refers to the variation in prices among yard sales, antique shops, and quilt show vendors. It also refers to the price differences from one area of the country to another. You need to be aware of this and adjust your budget accordingly. It's a good idea to scout the area in which you're shopping to get a ballpark figure for old quilt tops. As a point of information, the old quilt tops shown in this book cost between $15 and $120.

Having a budget doesn't necessarily mean you must stick slavishly to it, though. You may (in rare cases) spend less than the amount you budgeted, or (as is far more likely) you may be faced with deciding whether you will spend more than you budgeted. When we plan for these purchases, we settle on what we're willing to pay (a round figure) and then add $10 to $15 as a cushion that we're willing to add to the top price if we simply can't pass up a special top. Of course, it is possible to rationalize any purchase if you concentrate on it!

As with everything else, there are catches in the purchasing of these old tops, so ask yourself if it's really feasible to complete any given top you are considering buying.

Are all, or at least most, of the fabrics in relatively good shape? Check for fabric fading or rotting. If any fabrics need replacing, what will you replace them with and where will you get it?

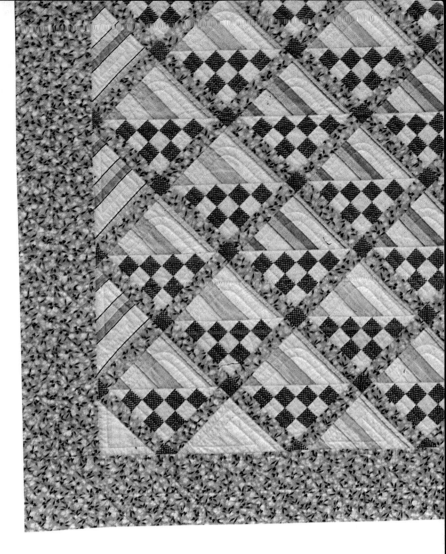

Do you like the colors, pattern, and fabrics? If you complete it, do you have a reasonable expectation that you will be pleased with it? This all boils down to asking yourself if buying and completing a particular top is worth your time, money, and effort. However, do avoid asking advice from friends who are not sympathetic to these kinds of projects, for such friends are dangerous!

After considering your budget and the other factors involved, there is one overwhelming reason for choosing a top and that is: you must like the piece or no matter how terrific the completed top turns out to be, all of your time, money, and effort will be poorly spent. You want this to be an enjoyable activity and not a punishment. Remember to listen to whether your heart is singing or if you have a big grin on your face—the tops that elicit these reactions are, all things being equal, the ones for you. If the piece makes Julie (one of our vendor friends) turn green, we most likely will want it.

CHAPTER 3

ADVANCE PREPARATION

Once you have the quilt top in hand, the first order of business is to take a photograph of it. Don't worry about the fact that you're probably not the world's greatest photographer; you've no need to try for a wonderful art photograph. What you're doing here is documenting the top as purchased. You can take color slides or color prints, whichever you are more comfortable with. Try to fill the view finder with the quilt to avoid extraneous background things showing on the sides of the quilt. Be sure to take more than one shot of the top so you can choose the best one for your full documentation. Don't forget to also take plenty of close-ups. When photographing these pieces be sure they are not being held by friends or relatives. Remember you want the photo of the quilt, not the quilt with fingers and legs. At this point, and before you do anything else, have the film processed to be certain you have some decent shots. If you take your film to a shop that offers one-hour processing for color prints, this step of the procedure won't delay, by much, the beginning of the actual quilt work. If you take color slides, it usually takes about a week to get them back. Remember, if you take prints, you can always have slides made from them, and vice versa.

After you have some clear slides or prints, it's time to wash the quilt top. Do this carefully, gently, and by hand. You can do this in a stationary tub or bathtub, but it is also possible to do this in the washing machine without agitation. This is considerably easier on the back and provides a more thorough washing. We would suggest using a laundering product such as Orvus Quilt Soap which was developed specifically for washing quilts. Most shops carry this or other non-phosphate detergent and quilt soaps, or can order it for you. If there isn't a quilt shop reasonably close to where you live, you can order this item through the mail (see the Resource List). After washing, be sure to rinse the top thoroughly. It is possible to put the top through the spin cycle. To dry, drape the top across two outdoor or indoor clotheslines (this eases the strain on the top) which are 15″ to 20″ apart. If hanging outside, these lines should not receive direct sunlight, or you can put your top out when the sun moves and the lines are in the shade. The piece can also be dried, if it is in good condition, in your dryer: use the delicate cycle on low heat. Remove the top before it is totally or overly dry and finish drying it on a flat surface. It is worth noting that some quilt conservators are against washing an old quilt top, but neither of us are interested in working with a dirty top, so we always wash them.

You need to be aware that at some time one of your purchases may not survive the washing process. You simply have to be philosophical about this and realize you didn't thoroughly inspect the top before purchasing it and that it was in much worse shape than you had thought. Even here, however, there is a silver lining because you can save the surviving pieces to use in the repair of another quilt top.

If the top is in reasonably good condition but smelly, wash and dry it and then, if the smell remains, place the unfolded top in a plastic bag with an unwrapped bar of Safeguard soap. Tie the bag shut. The size of the top and the degree of the odor determine the length of time the quilt needs to be kept in the bag to rid it of the smell. After a couple of days, check on the freshness of the top and continue the process as necessary. At

this point, document the quilt top as purchased and keep this material with the "before" photograph. Write a detailed description of the piece including the colors used, pattern name (and name variations), cost, and source. The documentation should also contain the size, date (or approximate date), and provenance (if you have it, or are able to obtain it). Add any other information that would be helpful in providing a full background for the piece. Don't forget to include the title you have given to the completed quilt.

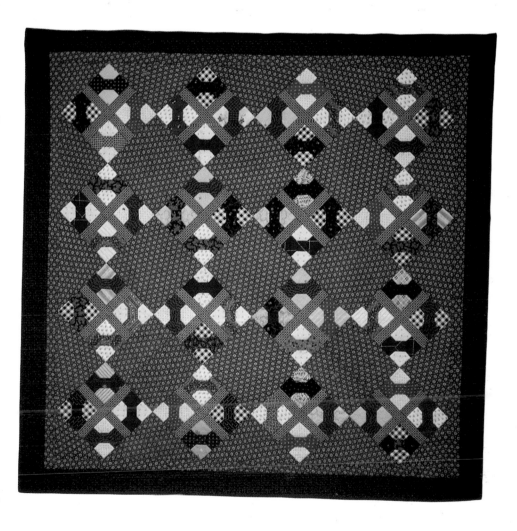

CHAPTER 4

SUPPLY LIST

When approaching any quiltmaking project, there are certain tools, supplies, and equipment you will need to make the work go smoothly. Here's a list for our projects plus some optional items:

1/8″ PAPER PUNCH: This tool is used to punch small holes in templates. The templates have the seam allowances included, and when marking around them, a circle is marked in the punched holes. These circles are then connected and the resultant lines are the sewing lines.

1/4″ MACHINE FOOT (Optional): Using this foot for machine work helps to maintain a consistent 1/4″ seam allowance when piecing. It makes life easier for the machine operator and is well worth the small investment if one didn't come with your machine.

BAND-AIDS: If you, like many quilters, tend to be a klutz or have a klutzy day from time to time, it's always good to keep a couple of these in your sewing basket.

BASTING SAFETY PINS: These are used to hold the three layers of the quilt together during the quilting process. Use them instead of thread basting the layers together. Size #1 non-rusting safety pins are the pins of choice. They are big enough to hold the three layers firmly together, but not so big as to make holes.

BATTING: Choose the batting you like to work with the most. For old quilt tops, cotton or wool batts are probably most suitable. However, a blend or a polyester batt can be used. The blend batt works well for machine quilting, and the polyester batt works well for hand quilting. For old quilts you will want to use a relatively low loft batt. All of the pieces presented here were done with a blend batt. One of the blend batts is Cotton Classic by Fairfield Processing Co.; it is 80% cotton and 20% polyester, with a low loft and a rough surface that grips the fabric. Another blend batt is Cotton Choice by Mountain Mist; it is 90% cotton and 10% polyester. Fairfield also makes Soft Touch, which is a 100% cotton, needle-punched batt. One of the 100% polyester batts is Thermore, by Hobbs, which is an ultra-thin batt. Another 100% polyester batt is Quilt Lite by Mountain Mist, and yet another is Traditional Batting by Fairfield.

BINDING CLIPS: These are used to hold the quilt binding securely in place as you hand stitch it to the back of the quilt. These prevent the stitcher from being jabbed as frequently happens when the binding is pinned in place.

COTTON THREAD: For hand work, match the thread color to the fabric color (if piecing two vastly different colors of fabric, match the thread color to the darker fabric). For machine work, use a neutral color thread; try either a medium gray or a medium tan. For quilting, choose the color (or colors) that most enhances the quilt top design or that doesn't interfere with it. More than one color of thread can be used for the quilting. Keep in mind that if the thread color matches the fabric color, any errors will be less obvious than if a contrasting color thread is used. Cotton thread is used because it is the thread least likely to damage the quilt's cotton fabric.

EMBROIDERY HOOP: If you are making or repairing embroidered blocks for a quilt top, use a solid, secure hoop of the correct size to hold the fabric during the embroidery process.

EVEN-FEED/PLAID-MATCHER/WALKING FOOT ATTACHMENT (Optional): This foot can make a world of difference in the results you achieve when machine quilting your piece. Find one that fits your machine and practice using it. It feeds the layers through evenly and helps prevent unacceptable pleats, bubbles, and the like in your work.

EXTENSION CORD (Optional): This will allow you to work on your sewing machine without being right on top of an outlet.

FABRIC SCISSORS: Use a good pair of sharp scissors for cutting fabrics. Use these scissors only for cutting fabric and not for cutting anything else. We have found Gingher's to be the best scissors on the market.

HAND NEEDLES: These are used for all hand sewing and sometimes are needed for details and finishing on machine-made quilts. Whether the work is piecing, appliqué, or quilting, use the type of needle in the size you find most comfortable. There is no law anywhere that says you must use quilting needles for quilting if you find sharps better for you. Remember: the higher the number, the finer the needle. It is, however, a good idea to use embroidery needles for embroidery work merely because they have a large eye which facilitates threading the floss, and size #8 is a good all purpose embroidery needle.

IRON: Use a good, heavy iron that has a steam function and, if possible, a spray function.

IRONING BOARD OR SURFACE: Use a standard ironing board with a good pad (a single cotton cover with a towel over it). Ironing boards that are the same generous width from one end to the other are even better than this. A small ironing board with short legs is handy to have on a table close to your sewing machine. A padded ironing surface can be folded up and carried anywhere and, again, it's handy to have on a table close to your machine.

MACHINE NEEDLES: Obviously, these are used for machine work. It's important to use the size needle that your operator's manual tells you is needed for that machine and the type of fabric you are using.

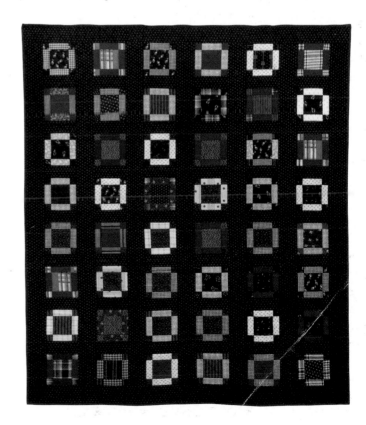

MAGIC SIZING: This supply is made by the Faultless Starch Company and is available at supermarkets. It is used to spray the fabric pieces as you press them. This product gives body to the fabric pieces and makes it easier to mark and sew them. If this is not available, try some spray starch.

MARKING TOOLS: Always test the marking tool on the fabric being used. For piecing, mark lightly with a regular pencil on light fabric, and on dark fabric use Berol Karismacolor in silver, lemon yellow, or pink (this medium is supposed to be water soluble). The other choices of colored pencils are Berol Prismacolor and Berol Verithin, both of which are permanent. For appliqué, use the same tools as for piecing. For quilting, use a regular pencil lightly on light fabric. On dark fabric, a Chakoner with white powered chalk is the preferred tool, but it is temporary. A Silver Berol Karismacolor pencil

can also be used, or draw the quilting design on medium weight interfacing (not iron-on), cut it out, baste it to the quilt, and quilt around it. For gentle curves and stems, you might consider basting white bias tape into the desired shape on the quilt top and quilting along it. Masking tape can be applied to the basted sandwich and quilted along the edge. Just don't leave the masking tape on for any length of time.

MASKING TAPE: This is one of those all-purpose supplies that can be used for a multitude of chores. It can hold your template material securely to the pattern and the template to the fabric. It can be used to affix notations to the template, or just stuck on a clear plastic template to make it easier to see. Masking tape can hold the backing securely and squarely to a flat surface for basting, can be used as a guide for quilting a straight line, and it can have your name written on it and be stuck to your tools.

NEEDLE THREADER: Whether as a help for your eyes or to get thread through the needle eye when you're working with fine needles that have tiny eyes, this tool can save lots of frustration.

ORVUS PASTE: This product is very good for washing your quilt tops and quilts. It is available at quilt shops or by mail order.

PENCIL SHARPENER: Whenever using a standard type pencil (as opposed to an automatic one), be it a "lead" or a colored pencil, keep a pencil sharpener handy so your marking tool is always very sharp and you can make a fine, light line on the fabric. A battery-operated sharpener has proved to be a good piece of equipment.

PERMANENT MARKING PEN: These can be used to make a label for your quilt, add any detailing you might wish to your quilt top, and to mark your template plastic. They come in a variety of colors and point sizes.

ROTARY CUTTER (Optional): This tool is available in a variety of sizes (the largest size seems to work best), is extremely sharp, and is most helpful in cutting alternate plain blocks, background blocks for appliqué, sashing, borders, and binding. Use with care to avoid miscutting (and wasting) fabric and yourself. Always retract the blade when you are not in the actual process of using it. We have found that the Olfa cutter is relatively easy to control.

ROTARY CUTTING MAT: This is a self-healing mat that is used with a rotary cutter. It protects your table surface and, because it is incrementally marked (most mats are), it helps square up and measure your fabric for cutting. These are available in various sizes, but the 17″ x 23″ mat is a good workable size.

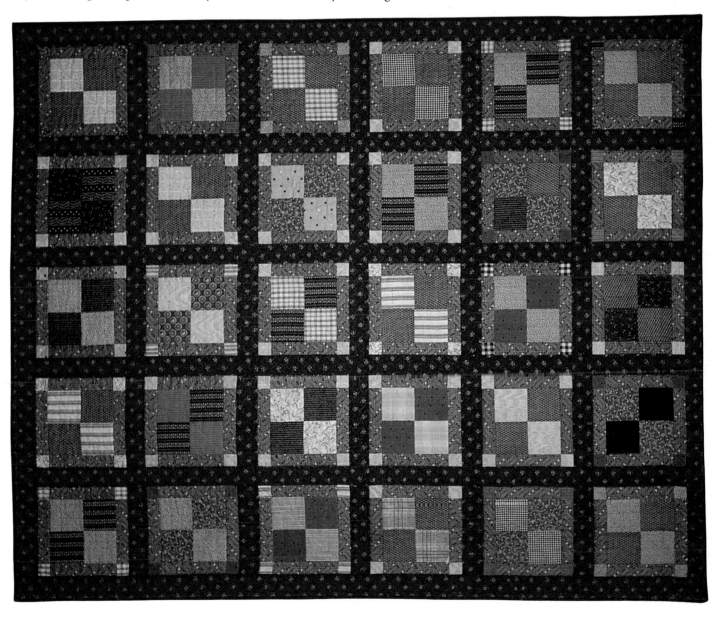

ROTARY CUTTING RULER (Optional): These thick acrylic or Plexiglas rulers come in a variety of styles, shapes, and sizes. They are incrementally marked, plus some of them have marks for cutting a selection of angles. These rulers are used in conjunction with a rotary cutter and a rotary cutting mat. Obviously, they can be used for plain old measuring, too.

RULER: Use one accurate ruler throughout the process of working on a single project. Depending on what is being measured, choose a 12″, 18″, or 24″ ruler.

SAFETY PIN CLOSER (Optional): This tool holds the sharp part of the safety pin off the quilt sandwich while you close the pin. If you are the type of stitcher who stabs yourself with needles and pins on a regular basis, this gadget might prove helpful.

SANDPAPER: Fine sandpaper is a great help in marking fabric for piecing and appliqué. Place the sandpaper, rough side up, on a flat surface, put the fabric on the sandpaper, and then use the template on the fabric while marking. To keep the sandpaper flat, purchase a large (about 12″ square) flexible floor tile with a peel-off backing, peel off the backing, and replace it with the sandpaper.

SEAM RIPPER: Have a couple of sharp seam rippers available. They will be used to remove stitching in areas where you must replace fabrics, or to do any repair work that requires cutting seams.

SEWING MACHINE (Optional):

All of the patterns presented here can be successfully executed by hand and most of them can be efficiently done by machine. Even if the entire piece is accomplished by hand, you will most likely use the machine to attach the binding to the top of the quilt and to construct the sleeve.

STRAIGHT PINS: Use these for holding pieces in place until they are sewn.

TEMPLATE MATERIAL: Use the material with which you are most comfortable working. If in doubt, a light-weight plastic is the best choice. It is the easiest to mark and cut, but firm enough to draw around without wearing down.

THIMBLE: Be sure to get a thimble that fits you well. If your fingers tend to swell from time to time for whatever reason, you might need two thimbles, for instance a size #8 and a size #9, to accommodate this situation. Use whatever type you prefer: leather, base metal, stretchable fabric, sterling, or gold.

THREAD CLIPPERS: These are snips or small scissors that can be used to clip threads as you work. It is better to use these than your large fabric scissors because there is less of a chance of cutting into your project with the smaller clippers, or for that matter, cutting into yourself.

UTILITY SCISSORS: A sharp pair of all-purpose scissors can be used to cut paper, cardboard, sandpaper, plastic, and other template materials. Do not use these scissors to cut fabric.

ASSESSING THE TOP

Once all of the advance preparation is completed, it's time to begin the actual work on the top. The first step is to determine the extent of the damage to the quilt top, if any. Look the piece over very carefully, scrutinizing every detail. You wouldn't want to overlook a problem only to have it turn up when the project is finished.

Be on the lookout for: 1) the integrity of every piece of fabric in the top: are some pieces faded, are some deteriorating, are some too loosely woven or too heavy, are others brittle (if so, they will tear), what is the quality of the fabric overall; 2) any stains or spills and how many of the pieces are affected by them; 3) how well are the pieces stitched together; 4) are the pieces consistent in size; 5) what was used to stitch the pieces (thread, floss, string) and how is it holding up; 6) does the top lie flat; 7) are all of the outside edges straight; 8) are selvages used; 9) if sashing and/or a border is used, are they of an appropriate size in relation to the other elements of the quilt top and to each other; 10) is there excessive puckering; 11) are the seam allowances adequate; 12) are there any marks (pencil, pen, etc.); 13) is there sufficient contrast in the fabric values to emphasize the pattern design; 14) do any embellishments need eliminating, repair, or replacing; 15) are there any holes.

Almost certainly one or more of these problems will appear in your quilt top and will have

to be dealt with before the piece is sandwiched for quilting. If the damage or problem appears in most areas of the quilt, if some of the fabrics are unusable, or if the piece won't lie flat, you will need to start from scratch so the problem areas can be removed.

Let's take a close-up look at the problems in the quilts presented in this book and what solutions were applied to the problems. Note: In most instances the completed quilts are somewhat smaller than the original tops. Also, the "as purchased" dates given are approximations, except for Susie Bell, which was made in 1932.

*B*ERTHA

"Bertha" (Flying Geese) was completely unusable as it was purchased, although most three-piece "Flying Geese" units were kept together. All of the quilt seams were picked out, and the pieces were remarked and restitched with some fabric used in the strip set being borrowed from another old quilt top of the same period. When being reassembled, the quilt top was machine pieced and the quilt was machine quilted. As purchased, the quilt top was 62″ x 75″. When renovation was complete, the quilt was 52″ x 64″.

Top: Late 1930s-1940s
As Purchased

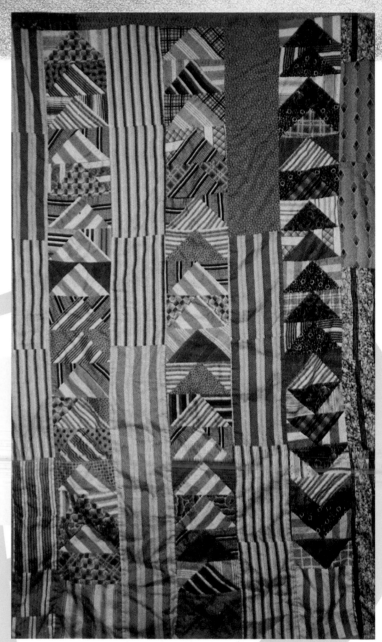

Quilt: 1992 by Jeannette T. Muir
As Completed

BLANCHE

"Blanche" (Square in a Square) was also in a sad condition when purchased. All of the parts were cut apart and then recut and restitched into a new strip setting. The borders were cut from the original large blue alternating blocks. In the reconstruction process, Blanche was machine pieced and machine quilted. Starting out at 70″ x 90″, it finished at 44″ x 60″.

Top:
1880–1900
As Purchased

Quilt: 1993 by Jeannette T. Muir
As Completed

ELIZABETH FLORENCE

"Elizabeth Florence" (Nine Patch Variation) had a large number of areas which had spills on them and, just as a guess, the spills appeared to be shellac. All of the pieces were unstitched and then recut and restitched. Some of the replacement squares in this piece are from other old tops of the same period. Because of the bad condition, and the need for replacement fabrics and their availability, the remade blocks ended up 5″, which is smaller than the original 6-1/2″ size. The original setting had forty-nine blocks set with seven blocks down and seven across. As completed, the set has forty-eight blocks set with eight blocks down and six across. The piecing and quilting were both done by machine. As purchased, the top was 72″ x 76″ and as completed 51″ x 59″.

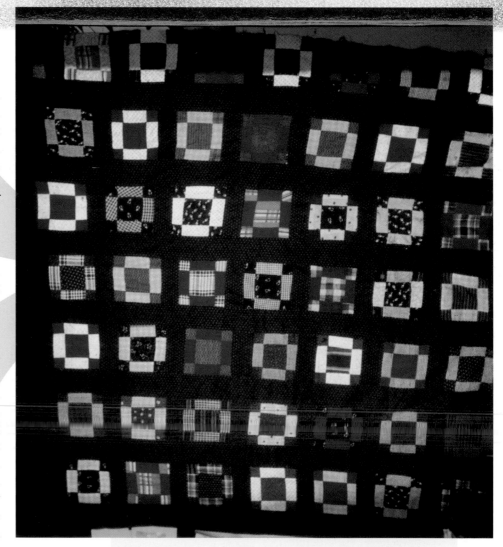

Top: 1880–1910
As Purchased

Quilt: 1998 by Jeannette T. Muir
As Completed

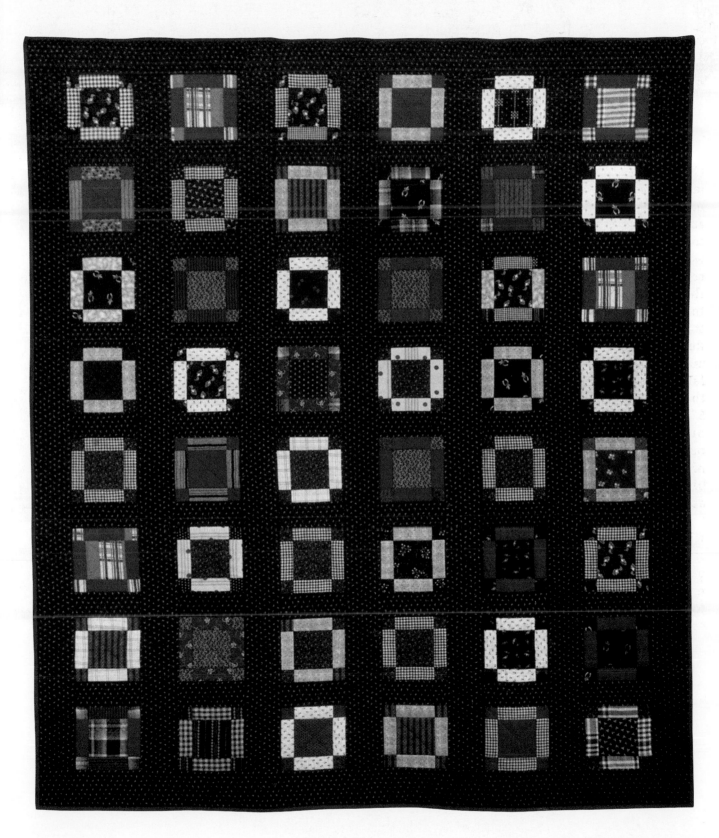

ELSIE MILDRED

"Elsie Mildred" (Four Patch Variation) had both stitching and construction details that were pathetic, the pieces were not consistent in size, it was badly stained, and to top it off, the pieces were stitched with string. Because of all of these problems, the entire top was picked apart, recut, and restitched. All of the fabrics used in the reconstruction of the top are original to the piece, and it was repieced by machine. The blocks were quilted by hand and the sashing and border were quilted by machine. Starting at 65″ x 78″, this quilt finished at 57″ x 68″.

Top:
1890–1910
As Purchased

Quilt: 1992 by Jeannette T. Muir
As Completed

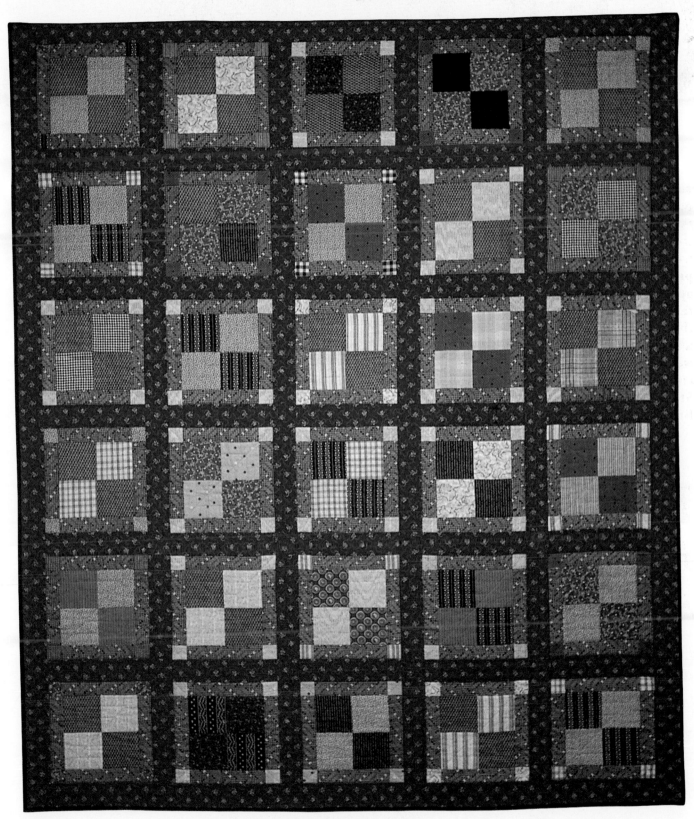

$\mathcal{E}$RNESTINE

"Ernestine" (King David's Crown) was in overall poor condition, and the entire top was taken apart. The pieces were recut, remarked, and restitched by hand. The red center squares in the completed quilt are replacements for the originals. Some fabrics in the blocks were replaced using fabrics of the same period. The original muslin was replaced with new blue fabric and a border of this same blue fabric was added. During the reconstruction of the pieced top, the work was done by hand, while the completed piece was machine quilted. The final quilt has the same number of blocks (fifty-six) as it did when purchased. The top was 70″ x 80″, and the quilt is 74″ x 84″ (this larger size is attributable to the addition of the border).

Top:
1930s–1940s
As Purchased

Quilt: 1993 by Jeannette T. Muir
As Completed

$\mathcal{F}$LORENCE

"Florence" (Pieced Baskets) was badly stained when purchased, and the selvages were included in the seam allowances. All of the top's pieces were taken apart, recut, and restitched, and all of the muslin was replaced. The repiecing and the quilting were done by machine. The original size of the piece was 74″ x 82″ and after reconstruction it measures 44″ x 52″.

Top:
1920s–1930s
As Purchased

Quilt: 1994 by Jeannette T. Muir
As Completed

HARRIET JOSEPHINE

"Harriet Josephine" (Eight-Pointed Star Variation) had both technical and visual problems. The muslin was badly stained and loosely woven, so it had to be replaced. The entire top was taken apart, recut, remarked, and restitched. In many of the blocks there was little contrast between the parts of the star. To remedy this, some of the fabrics were switched around among the star blocks. Borders were added and augmented with some of the original sashing pieces. The piecing was done by hand and the quilting by machine. New blue reproduction fabric was used in the border. Out of the sixty-four original diamonds, fifty-three were replaced. The blocks were redrafted down from 18″ x 18″ to 16″ x 16″ and with all of the adjustments, the 85″ x 95″ top finished at 79″ x 79″.

Top: 1930s-Early 1950s
As Purchased

Quilt: 1998 by Jeannette T. Muir
As Completed

HAZEL SOPHIA

"Hazel Sophia" (Harrison Rose—a Mountain Mist Pattern) had a major problem—its top was poor-quality muslin. The entire top was taken apart, reshaped, and the designs restitched on new muslin. Some of the fabrics were replaced with same-period fabrics in this process. The original sawtooth border was augmented with same-period fabrics and a plain border was added. It was both appliquéd and quilted by machine. The size of the piece started at 70″ x 86″ and ended at 62″ x 78″.

Top:
1910–1930s/1940s

As Purchased

Quilt: 1994 by Jeannette T. Muir
As Completed

IDA CAROLINE

"Ida Caroline" (Nine Patch) didn't lie flat, and some of the fabrics were not good. The entire top was picked apart, recut, and restitched. A few fabrics were replaced with same-vintage fabrics and a border of new fabric was added. Both the piecing and the quilting were done by machine. The original size was 72″ x 72″ and it ended up 64″ x 64″.

Top:
1880–1900

As Purchased

Quilt: 1998 by Jeannette T. Muir
As Completed

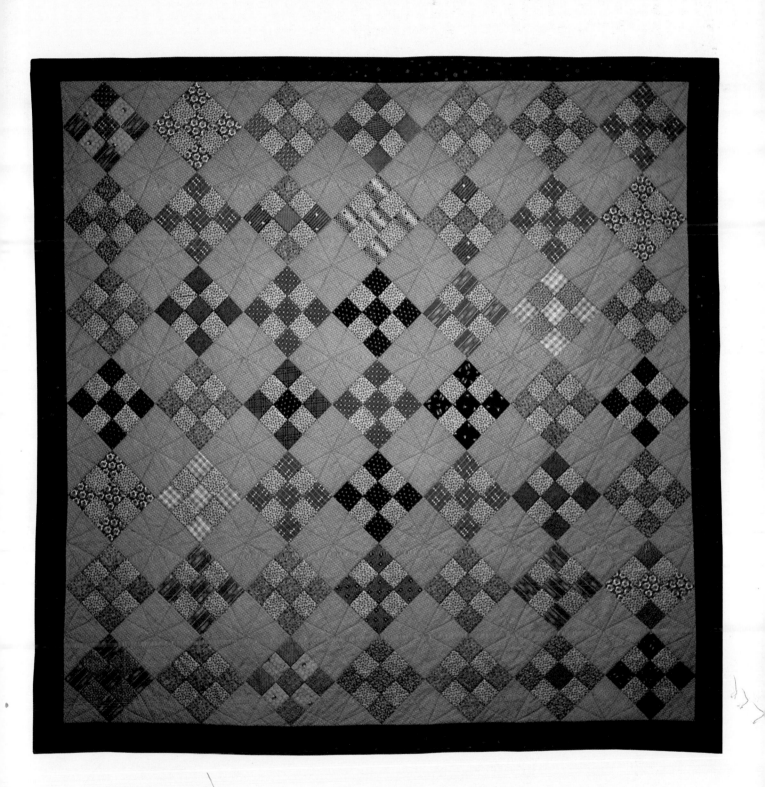

JEANNETTE

"Jeannette" (Pot of Flowers) had its biggest problem with the fabrics not being in good condition. All of the blocks were picked apart and recut to a consistent size. The original alternate blocks were replaced with new muslin. Most of the circular flower centers and a few flowers were replaced with same-vintage fabrics. Two new borders were added: a sawtooth border and a muslin border. The motifs were hand done and the entire work was machine quilted. The top was originally 59″ x 74″ and it finished at 75″ x 90″.

Top: 1930s
As Purchased

Quilt: 1994 by Jeannette T. Muir
As Completed

JENNY DELL

"Jenny Dell" (Bow Tie) was completely taken apart, and some fabrics in the blocks were replaced using same-vintage fabrics. It was machine pieced, and while the pattern blocks were hand quilted, everything else was machine quilted. There were twenty blocks in the original 70″ x 86″ work, and after repair and reconstruction there are sixteen blocks in the 61″ x 61″ work.

Top:
1890–1915

As Purchased

Quilt: 1998 by Jeannette T. Muir
As Completed

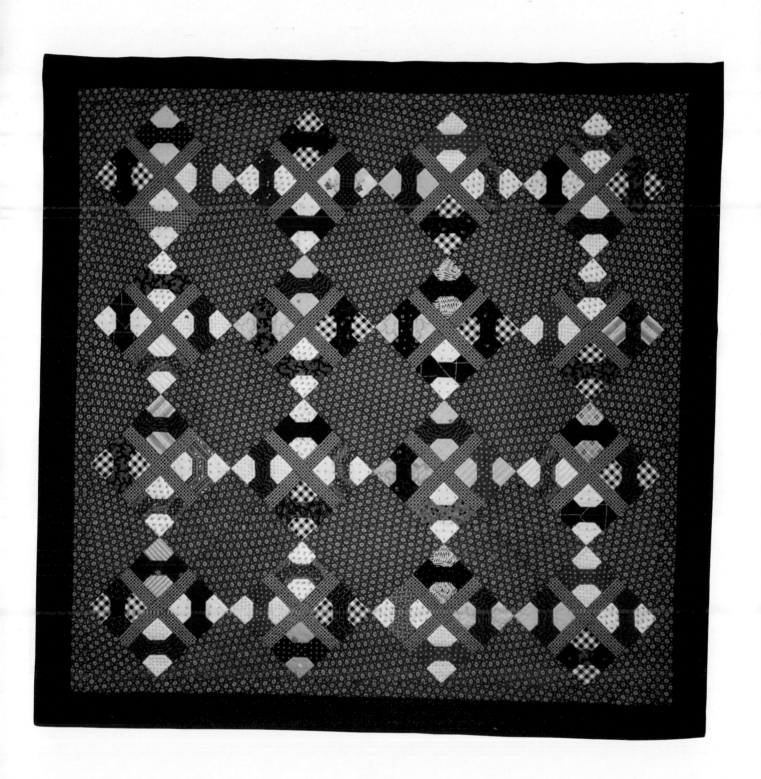

JESSIE

"Jessie" (Honeycomb) was reshaped from a large overall hexagon to a rectangle. Some fabrics were replaced with vintage fabrics, the center pattern was appliquéd to new muslin to provide straight sides, and a border was added. It was hand pieced using the English piecing technique and it was machine quilted. Starting with an original size of 78″ x 78″ x 78″ from point to point, the piece was completed at 62″ x 85″.

Top: 1930s

As Purchased

Quilt: 1994 by Jeannette T. Muir
As Completed

KIRTLEY

"Kirtley" (St. Andrew's Cross) was the simplest quilt top to prepare for quilting because its only problem was severely ruffled borders. The borders were taken off, cut to size, and reattached. The entire piece was machine quilted except for the red fabric which was hand quilted. In this case, the original size was 85″ x 85″, and the finished size is 85″ x 85″.

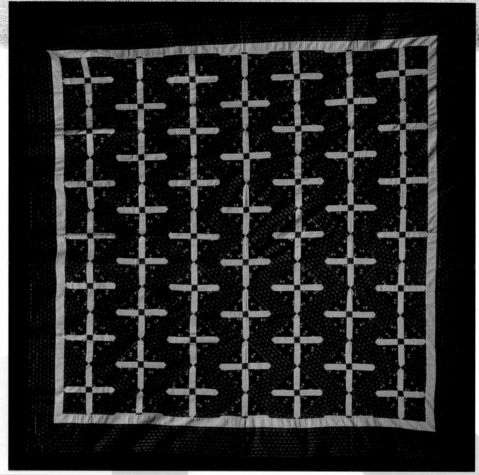

Top: 1880s–1900

As Purchased

Quilt: 1995 by Jeannette T. Muir
As Completed

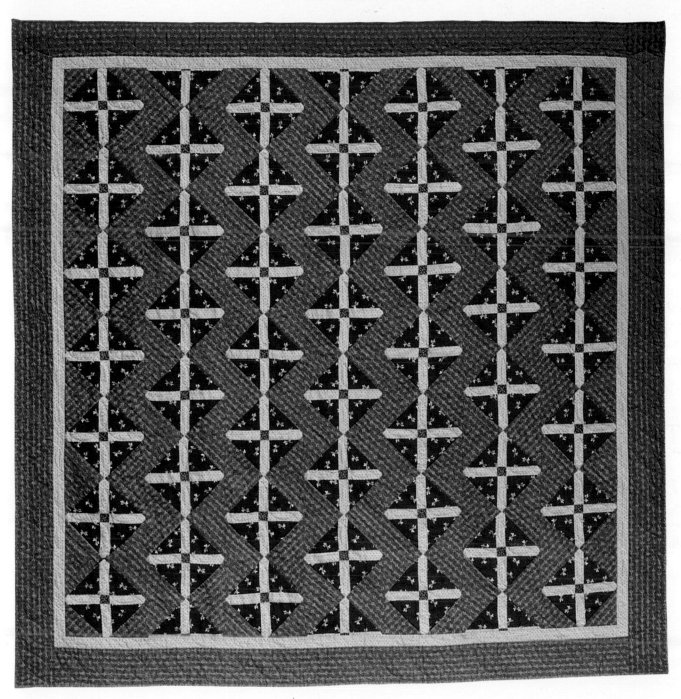

Nellie

"Nellie" (Embroidery) had its blocks taken apart from the sashing and border and cut from approximately 9″ x 9″ to a consistent size of 7-1/2″ x 7-1/2″. The sashing was cut down from 5″ wide to 2-1/4″ wide, and the border width was cut down. The prairie points were all cut from the original fabric left from cutting down the sashing and border. The blocks were hand embroidered using a limited number of stitches and then hand tied. The sashing and border were machine pieced in and then machine quilted. The original source for these patterns ("Cute Little Quilts for the Children") was Signe I. Pinch. They were available from the late 1920s to 1980 and were fabric blocks with the design stamped on them in color. The original size was 76″ x 74″, and the finished size is 52″ x 52″ with the prairie points (50″ x 50″ without them).

Top:
1920s–1930s
As Purchased

Quilt: 1996 by Jeannette T. Muir
As Completed

PRISCILLA

"Priscilla" (Milky Way) was made from scraps of vintage fabric left over from various old top renovations. This quilt was done using the paper piecing foundation technique. It was both machine pieced and quilted and is 47″ x 61″.

Top: 1910–1930s (scraps)

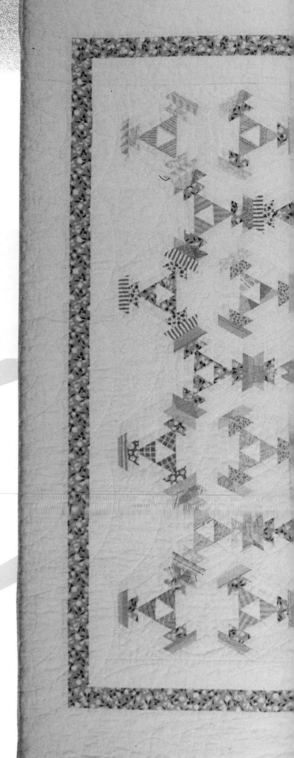

Quilt: 1997 by Jeannette T. Muir
As Completed

SUSIE BELL

"Susie Bell" (Appliquéd Animals) was made in 1932. In the original, the animals were blanket stitched with black embroidery floss, and the piece was tied with thick thread that made holes. Some fabric was replaced with same-vintage fabric. The sashing had deteriorated and was replaced with fabric from the original backing. All of the motifs were removed from the background blocks and reapplied on new muslin. The animal motifs are machine appliquéd to the new muslin and the blocks are hand quilted while the sashing and border are machine quilted. The starting size was 39″ x 53″, and it finished at 34-1/2″ x 50″.

Original Quilt: 1932
by Susie Bell Othick Denver
(Leftover Blocks)

Quilt: 1997 by Jeannette T. Muir
As Completed (From the collection of Cynthia Muir Preston)

THELMA

"Thelma" (Thousand Pyramids) is made mostly of flannel. The entire top was picked apart, recut, remarked, and restitched. One hundred of the pieces were unusable and were discarded because of bad condition (holes, paint, etc.). The border is new. The work was machine pieced and machine quilted. The original, at 86″ x 72″, was mostly hand pieced, and it finished at 56″ x 56″.

Top:
1880s–1900
As Purchased

Quilt: 1997 by Jeannette T. Muir
As Completed

VIDA

"Vida" (Four Patch) was taken apart, recut, and restitched. Eighty-six of the original pieces were replaced with fabric of the same vintage because some of the fabric originally used was inappropriate (slippery and loosely woven) while others had holes. The original set was maintained by using the original sashing and border. The work was machine pieced and machine quilted. Starting at 76″ x 76″, it finished at 64″ x 54″.

Top:
1880s–1900

As Purchased

Quilt: 1996 by Jeannette T. Muir
As Completed

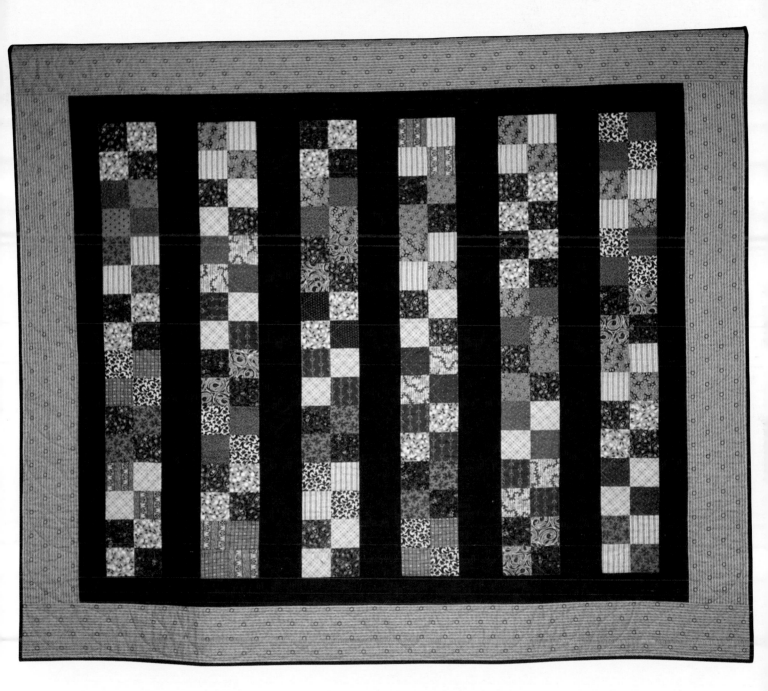

$\mathcal{Z}$AMA BELLE

"Zama Belle" (Colonial Basket) had fabric that was in terrible condition. All of the parts were picked apart, recut, and restitched. Some blocks were unusable; the original top had thirty blocks, and the finished quilt has twenty blocks. All original fabrics were used. The basket handles were reappliquéd, and the border was constructed from the leftover plain blocks. The work was hand pieced and both hand and machine quilted. At 63″ x 76″ when purchased, it finished at 39″ x 48″.

Top:
1880s–1900
As Purchased

Quilt: 1995 by Jeannette T. Muir
As Completed

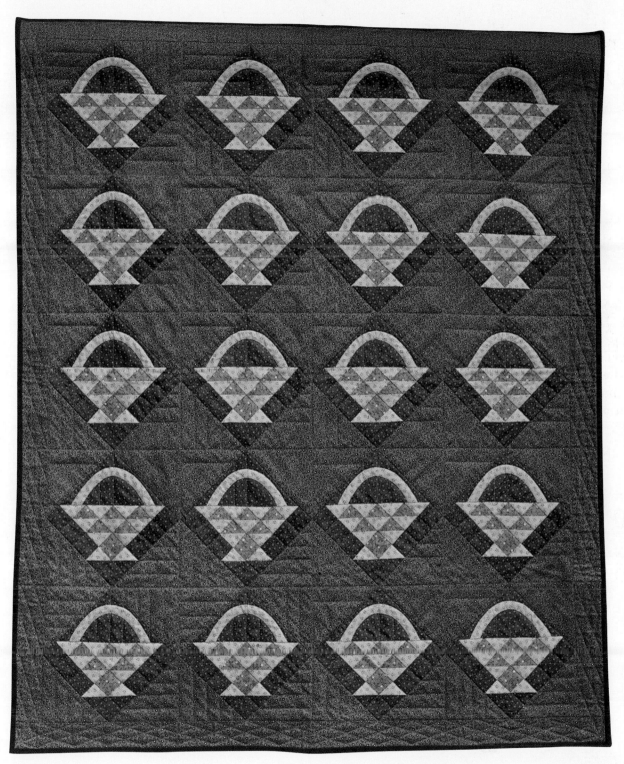

Having gone through all of the quilts, you now have some idea of the problems you can face when completing old quilt tops and some solutions for them. This is obviously not a pursuit for the impatient, but for those who persevere it is very rewarding.

CHAPTER 6

REMAKING THE TOP

Once you have carefully looked at the quilt top and know where the problems lie, it's time to begin the work. You may be lucky and merely have to remove, recut, and restitch a border as in Kirtley. On the other hand, it's far more likely that a more extensive repair job is in the offing and that you need to start all over again.

To start from scratch, unstitch the entire top. This may seem drastic if there are areas that don't seem to have any problems, but you will need all component parts of the project to be the correct and consistent size if you want the piece to lie/hang flat. It's better to spend extra time at this point and do a thorough job than to later wish you had.

There are some things to keep in mind as you take the quilt top apart, among them the quilt layout or set. If you don't want to make any changes in the "look" of the top, you will need to keep track of the pieces' original placements. Let's say, for instance, that the quilt top being worked on is composed of nine-patch blocks and alternate plain blocks. All of the nine squares for each block can be stacked and held together with a straight pin. Any of the squares that must be removed for any problem are replaced with another square. These replacement squares can, and preferably should, be of the same vintage as the rest of the fabric in the top. However, if this is not available to you, consider using reproduction fabric or at least contemporary fabric that has the "look" of the vintage fabrics in the top you're working on. The alternate plain blocks can also be stacked and pinned. Another method of keeping track of the placement is to use large squares of muslin, old sheets cut up, or whatever else is handy (even opened-up brown paper grocery sacks). Take apart the first quilt block and pin the pieces in their original order to the large square. Continue pinning the

pieces for each block to a separate large square until the top is completely taken apart. You can make any pertinent notes right on the cut square. The large squares can be used over and over for other projects. Still another method of keeping track of placement is for when you want a complete reference to the original: use an intact old sheet and pin every piece, as it is taken out of the quilt top, in its proper place on the sheet. You can also make a placement sketch, rely on your memory, use your pin-up wall (if you're fortunate enough to have one), or just put the pieces back together in an arrangement that is pleasing to you.

To pick the seams to get the top apart, use a seam ripper. Use this slowly and carefully to avoid damaging (or doing additional damage to) the top. This job will be easier if a heavy-duty, good-quality seam ripper is used.

· Once the entire top is taken apart, spray each piece on the right side with Magic Sizing (or lacking that, spray starch) and press it. Using this product keeps the fabric from being too soft and floppy (and thus difficult to work with).

Before you begin restitching, be sure you know how the top will be set because this may affect the stitching order. Generally speaking,

it's probably a good idea to maintain the original set. Sometimes, however, this is not possible (for whatever reason), and at other times changing the set can produce spectacular results, as shown in the before and after photos of Sarah Abigail (see pages 48 and 49). After all, this is now your top to handle as you wish so maintain or alter the set as you prefer.

The actual stitching of the quilt top can be done by hand or machine (except for the English piecing technique), or if you prefer, a mixture of the two. Many people like to stitch the blocks by hand and then add the sashing and border by machine. There is no problem in using both methods in one quilt top. There are two important things to keep in mind: 1) use cotton thread for the stitching no matter what sewing method is used (thread is covered in the Supply List), and 2) don't stitch in the seam allowances; leave them free to be pressed in the desired direction once the top is completed.

CHAPTER 7

Making the Quilt

Once the quilt top is reassembled, press it thoroughly and carefully and set it aside. It is now time to purchase your batting (see the Supply List) and your backing. For the backing you have your choice of using fabric of the same vintage as the top or of using new fabric. Possibly fabric of the same vintage would be the more appropriate, but there are several problems inherent in its use: 1) it is not readily available; 2) it is often loosely woven; 3) it is narrow; 4) in most cases it is cost prohibitive; and 5) it frequently is not strong enough to support the quilting.

On the other hand, new fabric is: 1) obviously readily available; 2) wide; 3) affordable within reason; 4) strong enough to stabilize the entire project; and 5) able to support the quilting. Allow yourself time to look at a variety of possible fabrics for this purpose; check more than one source and weigh all of the pros and cons of using both old and new fabric.

The backing fabric should be washed, pressed, and cut to size, seaming when necessary to get the proper size. It's a good idea to make the backing 2″ to 3″ bigger on all sides than the quilt top and to make the batting 1″ bigger.

Place the backing, right side down (wrong side up), on a large, flat surface. For most of us, this means the floor. Masking tape the backing smoothly, evenly, and squarely to the surface. On top of the backing, carefully lay out your chosen batting, smoothing it so it lies flat.

On top of this, place the well-pressed quilt top, again smoothing it so it lies totally flat.

The three layers can be thread basted together or they can be safety pin basted together (see the Supply List). The choice is yours, so use the method most comfortable for you.

The quilting pattern may be marked before or after basting (see the Supply List). Suggested quilting patterns accompany the patterns in the project section of the book (Chapter 9).

The quilting can be done by hand, by machine, or by a combination of the two methods. Again, cotton thread should be used, while the choice of thread color is a design decision you will have to make. Given these are old tops, white or ecru color thread would be a safe, if not a terribly exciting or interesting, choice.

Edge finishing is the last step in making the quilt. There are quite a few options open to the quiltmaker for the finishing: butted edges, back over front, front over back, insertions such as ruffles, pleats, and prairie points, and others. By far, however, the most often used method of edge finishing is double fold binding, cross grain or bias. Use the edge finishing method that you're most comfortable with and which gives you the best results. In addition to the choices of finishing methods, you have to make a decision on the fabric to use if you plan to bind the piece. Preferably, same vintage fabrics should be used, but lacking that, find the most compatible fabric that will not detract from the top or call undue attention to itself. Commercial bias binding is generally unacceptable because of its quality, color choices, and fiber content.

Even if the entire quilt is done by hand, it's probably a good idea to prepare the binding and stitch it to the top of the quilt by machine, then stitch it to the back of the quilt by hand. In preparing to bind the quilt, stitch around the

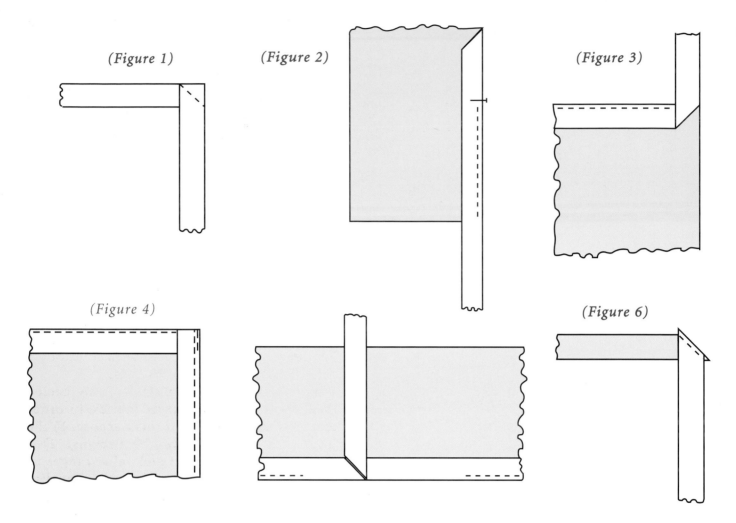

(Figure 1) (Figure 2) (Figure 3)

(Figure 4) (Figure 6)

entire perimeter of the project approximately 3/16″ from the edge using the walking foot (see the Supply List). Square up the corners and clean finish the edges using your rotary cutter, mat, and ruler. Cut 2-1/4″ strips across the width of the binding fabric to measure 10″ longer than the perimeter of the quilt. Stitch these pieces, right sides together, using diagonal seams (Figure 1) to get the length needed. Trim the seams and press them open, then cut one end at a 45° angle. Fold in half lengthwise, wrong sides together (right sides out), and press. Lay out the binding around the perimeter to be sure it is of sufficient size and to avoid seams at the corners by adjusting the starting/ending point. The starting point for applying the binding should be about the middle of the bottom edge of the piece. Leave the first 5″ of the binding unstitched (the end cut at an angle). Matching the raw edges of the binding to the raw edge of the quilt, stitch the binding to the quilt, working on the top side of the quilt. Stitch to within 1/4″ of the corner, backstitch, and remove from sewing machine,

clipping the threads only (Figure 2). Fold the binding (Figures 3 and 4) and stitch to the next corner. Repeat this procedure at all corners. Leave 5″ of the binding unstitched when nearing the original starting point. Pin the binding in place. Fold the end to match the angle. Mark this fold line (Figure 5). Unfold the binding and add 1/2″ to end beyond the first fold line, fold, and mark another line, then cut on this second fold line on each piece. Join the ends with a 1/4″ seam, matching folds (Figure 6). Press this seam open. Stitch the remaining section to the quilt top. Carefully smooth the binding to the back of the quilt and hand stitch it in place using matching-colored thread and mitering corners (top and back) as you work. Be sure to stitch the miters closed as you work on each corner. Be careful not to stretch either the quilt or the binding during the edge finishing. Don't forget that the binding should be completely filled with batting or that the batting should come all of the way to the edges if another method of finishing is used.

COMPLETING THE DETAILS

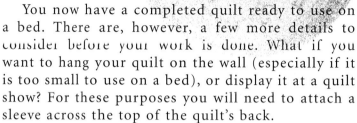

You now have a completed quilt ready to use on a bed. There are, however, a few more details to consider before your work is done. What if you want to hang your quilt on the wall (especially if it is too small to use on a bed), or display it at a quilt show? For these purposes you will need to attach a sleeve across the top of the quilt's back.

The first step in making a sleeve is to decide what fabric to use. There are three fabrics, in order of preference, that can work for this purpose: 1) the same fabric that was used for the backing; 2) a fabric that has the same color and value ranges as the top and the binding of the quilt; and 3) muslin. Be sure to wash the fabric before starting to make the sleeve.

A 4″ sleeve is generally the accepted and requested size for most quilt shows. To construct the sleeve, cut the fabric 9″ long by the width of the quilt, including binding, piecing if necessary to get the necessary width. Narrowly hem the short edges. Fold this piece in half lengthwise, wrong sides together, and stitch the long edges together with a 1/2″ seam. Turn the tube until the seam allowances run down the center of the tube; this is now the wrong, or back, side of the sleeve. Press the sleeve thoroughly, being careful to smoothly press the seam allowances open. Place the wrong, or back, side of the sleeve to the top back of the quilt just below the top binding and inside the side bindings and pin in place. Using matching-colored thread, hand stitch the sleeve securely in place, leaving the top layer of the sleeve unstitched at the ends, and being careful not to penetrate the top of the quilt with these stitches.

Some quiltmakers put an additional sleeve on the bottom of the quilt and place a rod in it to help the quilt hang flat and straight. Others may use

General Instructions

A consistent format is used for the presentation of projects, beginning with a brief description and a close-up of the quilt. The technique(s) involved is followed by suggested fabrics. Approximate yardage requirements, based on 42″ wide fabric, are given, but always purchase more than you need, just to be sure. This is called augmenting your inventory and is always a pleasure.

Directions are presented to assemble the tops like those pictured. Three levels of expertise are included: Basic, Intermediate, and Experienced. All of the patterns can be re-sized according to your needs. Be sure to adjust the yardage requirements as necessary.

Piecing, by hand or machine, is the primary technique used, and most of the projects can be pieced by machine, raw edge to raw edge. However, some of the projects, specifically "Harriet Josephine," "Jenny Dell," and "Ernestine," require the "precision" piecing method. Precision piecing is described as the old-fashioned method. Templates are needed, along with a sharp marking tool to mark a stitching line. The stitching is completed from circle to circle.

To prepare the templates, place the template material on top of the pattern. Using a permanent pen, transfer the dots, add the seam allowance, and cut on the outside cutting line. Punch out the dots with a 1/8″ paper punch.

When transferring the markings to the wrong side of the fabric, mark the entire circle. The circles are much more visible than just dots,

especially on the old fabric. (Sandpaper underneath the fabric will help prevent distortion.) Connect the dots using the template's straight edge. The edge of the template is also useful for scooping up the fabric from the sandpaper.

Pin fabrics, right sides together, matching seam lines and corresponding circles. Begin stitching the seam at one circle and stop at the other, leaving the seam allowances unstitched. If the seam is on the bias, take a backstitch every 1-1/2″, and every 2″ on a straight-of-grain or cross-grain seam, for strength.

What little appliqué is used in these projects was prepared using one of the freezer paper methods. Choose your favorite method; the options are enormous.

Most of the templates include a suggested grain placement arrow. Frequently we have no choice because the pieces in the old top dictate how they will be placed. Straight of grain at the sides, and cross grain at the top and bottom, is preferred so the quilt will hang, if applicable, or lie flat without ruffles.

Pressing is very important, especially in complicated projects. Some directions include arrows suggesting which way to press the seams. Generally, the initial seams are pressed toward the darkest fabric. Press as you go, by finger creasing or using a steam iron.

Many of these projects were hand pieced and the vast majority were machine quilted. Continuous-line quilting tracks are suggested—optional of course—and can be done by hand or machine, or even both.

Remember, there are no rules! Enjoy!

THE PROJECTS

BASIC

INTERMEDIATE

EXPERIENCED

BERTHA

(52″ x 64″)
(Basic)

A perennial favorite pattern, the "Flying Geese" units are set strippie style, separated by matching strips, or pieced strips using a variety of different fabrics.

Technique:
Piecing, by hand or machine

Fabrics:
A wide variety of light-colored and medium-colored prints

Approximate yardage:
1 yard light and 1 yard medium for the Flying Geese units
Total of 2 yards of many compatible fabrics, or one single fabric, for the long strips

Assembly:
1. *For each unit, as shown in Figure 1, cut one large triangle using Template A and two corner triangles using Template B. For variety, use the light and medium fabrics interchangeably for the Flying Geese units. The finished size of unit is 6-3/4″ x 3-1/8″. Press the seams toward the corners. Prepare seventy-two units.*

2. *Stitch completed units together in four vertical rows of eighteen.*

3. *Randomly piece together five 5-1/2″ strips to match the length of the vertical pieced rows.*

4. *Assemble in a strippie set as shown in Figure 2.*

Quilting:
The dotted lines in Figure 3 represent optional horizontal continuous-line quilting tracks.

Figure 1

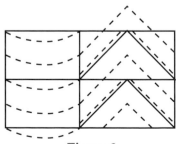

Figure 3

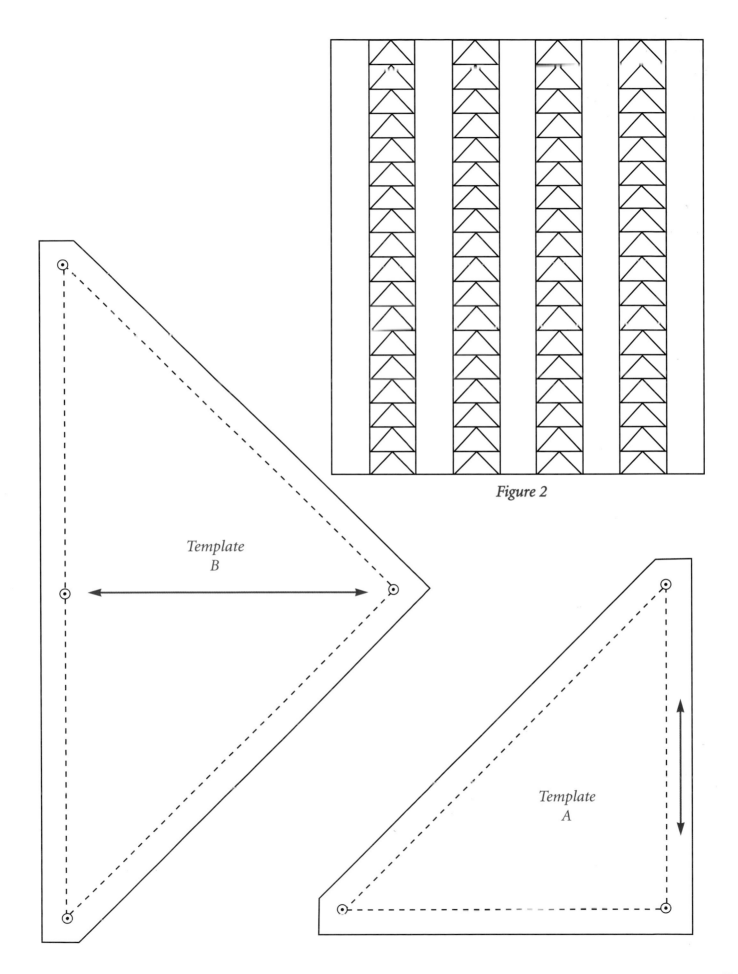

Figure 2

*Template
B*

*Template
A*

BLANCHE

(44″ x 60″)
(Basic)

"Square Within a Square" blocks are strippie set on point with alternating dark and light background triangles. For variety, interchange the light/dark combinations.

Technique:
Piecing (use templates)

Fabrics:
A wide variety of dark and medium scraps for the blocks; a variety of medium light and dark fabrics for the zigzag setting triangles; compatible fabric for the borders

Approximate yardage:
Total of 1-1/2 yards for the blocks
1-1/4 yards medium-light fabric for the setting triangles
1 yard assorted dark fabrics for the setting triangles
1-3/4 yards for the borders (these may be pieced, requiring less yardage)

Assembly:
1. For each block, cut one square using Template A and four triangles using Template B.

2. Assemble as shown in Figure 1 (need a total of thirty-three full-size blocks).

3. Prepare four half-blocks as shown in Figure 2.

4. Using Template C, cut twenty-eight dark setting triangles, thirty-six medium-light setting triangles, and twelve half-triangles (half of Template C) to place at the top and bottom of the medium light strips.

5. Place pieced blocks on a design wall, on point, in three vertical rows of seven and two vertical rows of six. Add setting triangles as shown in Figure 3. Audition as desired.

6. Assemble each strip diagonally as indicated in Figure 4.

7. Assemble the completed rows vertically.

8. Add 2-1/2″ borders, or personal preference.

Quilting:
The dotted lines in Figure 5 represent optional quilting tracks.

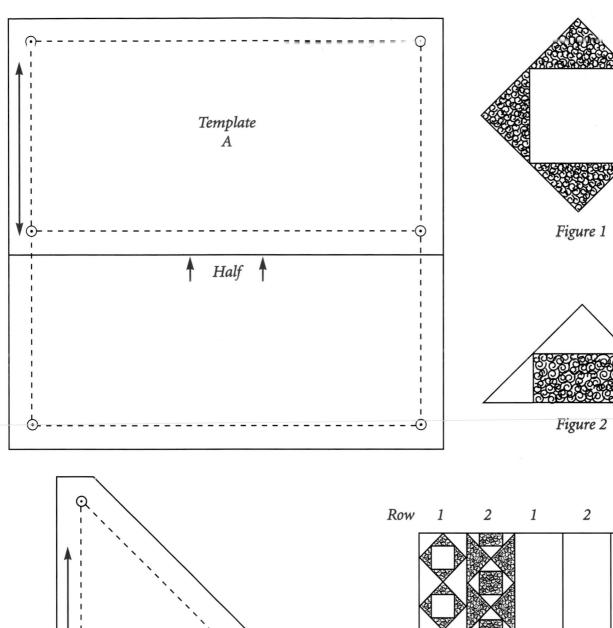

Template A

↕

↑ *Half* ↑

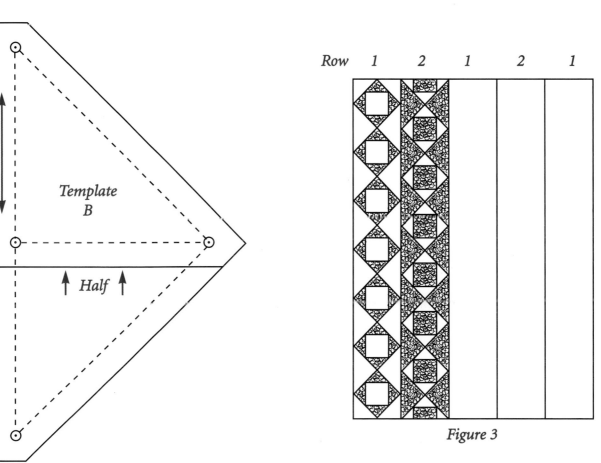

Template B

↕

↑ *Half* ↑

Figure 1

Figure 2

Row   1   2   1   2   1

Figure 3

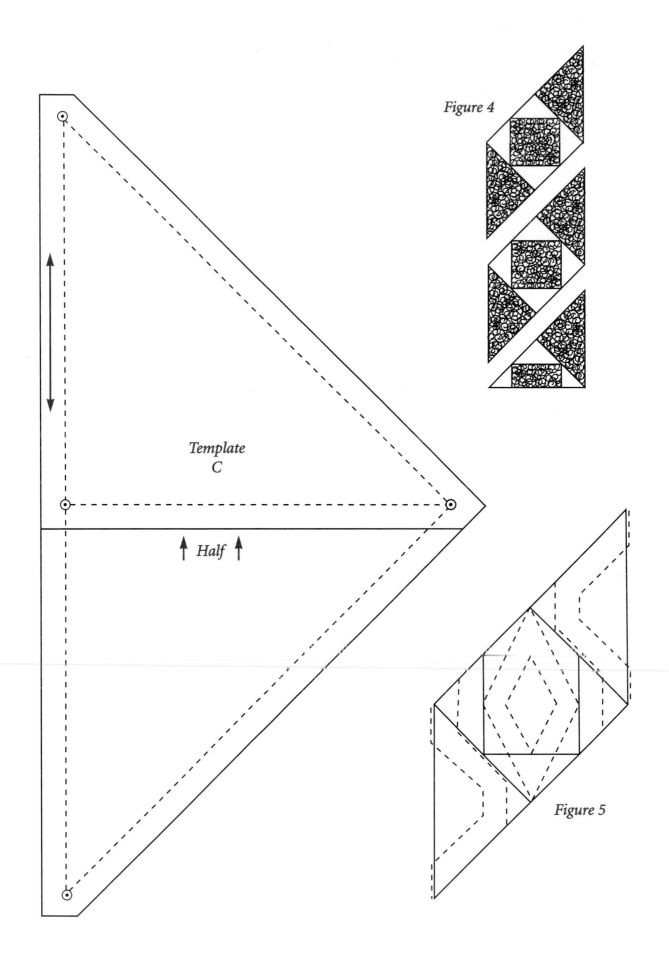

Figure 4

Template
C

↑ Half ↑

Figure 5

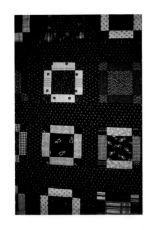

ELIZABETH FLORENCE

(51″ x 59″)
(Basic)

Unequal Nine-Patch blocks are straight set in vertical rows with long vertical sashing between.

Technique:
Piecing, by hand or machine (rotary cut or use templates)

Fabrics:
A wide variety of light, medium, and dark scraps; dark navy or indigo for the sashing and border

Approximate yardage:
Total of 1-1/2 yards light, medium, and dark scraps for the blocks
2 yards dark navy or indigo for the sashing and border

Assembly:
1. *For each 5″ (finished) block (Figure 1), cut one 3-1/2″ square, four 1-1/2″ x 3-1/2″ rectangles, and four 1-1/2″ squares, or use Templates A, B, and C.*

2. *Assemble as indicated in Figure 2. Numbers indicate the piecing sequence. Prepare forty-eight blocks.*

3. *Set in six vertical rows of eight blocks, separated by 2-1/2″ x 5-1/2″ sashing, or use Template D.*

4. *Cut five 3-1/2″ wide strips to match the length of the pieced vertical rows.*

5. *Assemble the rows as indicated in Figure 3.*

6. *Add a 3-1/2″ border, or personal preference.*

Quilting:
The dotted lines in Figure 3 represent optional continuous-line quilting tracks.

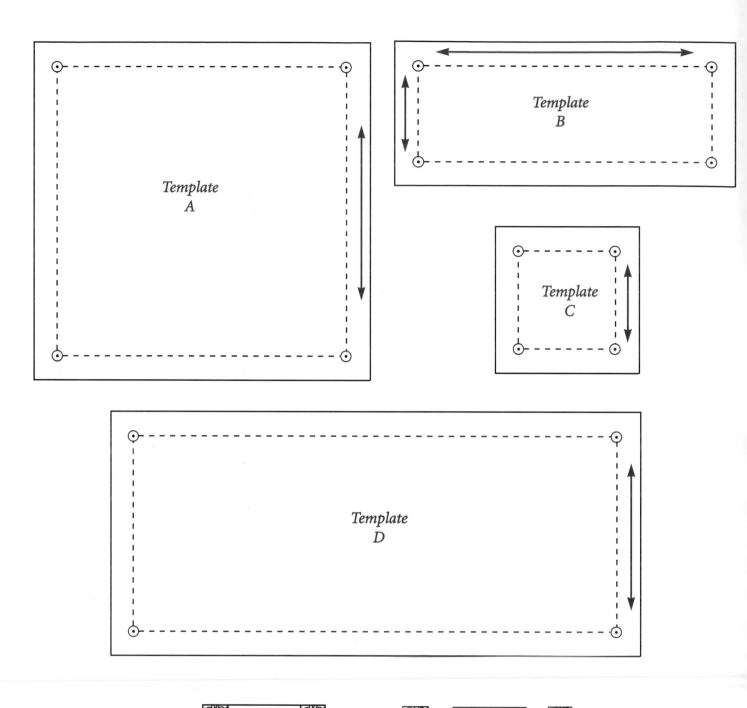

Template
A

Template
B

Template
C

Template
D

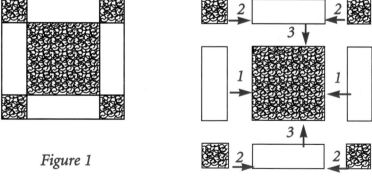

Figure 1

Figure 2

Figure 3

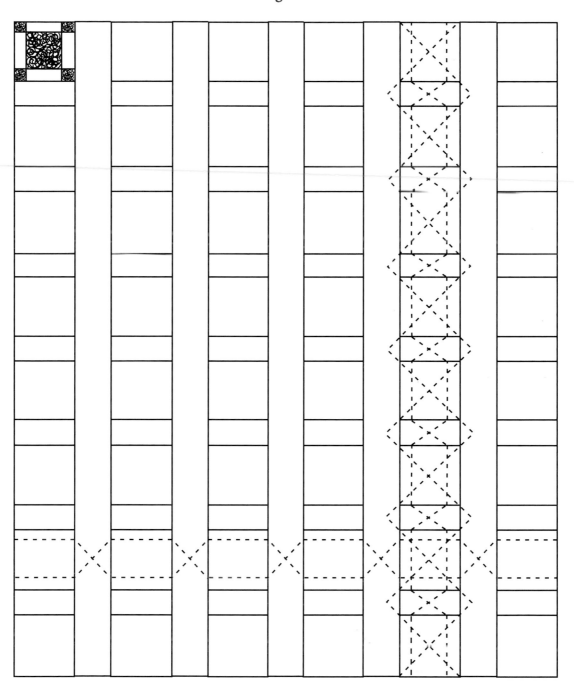

ELSIE MILDRED

(57" x 68")
(Basic)

Framed "Four Patch" blocks are straight set, five by six, and separated by sashing. Note: Because the original sashing fabric was delicate, individual "posts" were stitched between each block to strengthen the long strips.

Technique:
Piecing, by hand or machine (rotary cut or use templates)

Fabrics:
A wide variety of light and dark scraps for the squares; medium scraps for the frames; bright fabric for the sashing and border

Approximate yardage:
1 yard light scraps and 3/4 yard dark scraps
1 yard medium scraps for the frames
2 yards bright fabric for the sashing and border

Assembly:
1. For each block, cut two light 3-3/4" squares and two dark 3-3/4" squares, or use Template A.

2. Assemble as indicated in Figure 1.

3. Cut four frame pieces 7" x 1-3/4", or use Template B.

1. Cut four light 1-3/4" squares, or use Template C.

5. Following the numerical sequence, complete each block as shown in Figure 2. Prepare thirty blocks (9" finished).

6. Set blocks in six horizontal rows of five, adding 2½" (2" finished) sashing between blocks.

7. Stitch 2-1/2" (2" finished) sashing between rows.

8. Add 2" to 3" border, or personal preference.

Quilting:
The dotted lines in Figure 3 represent optional quilting tracks.

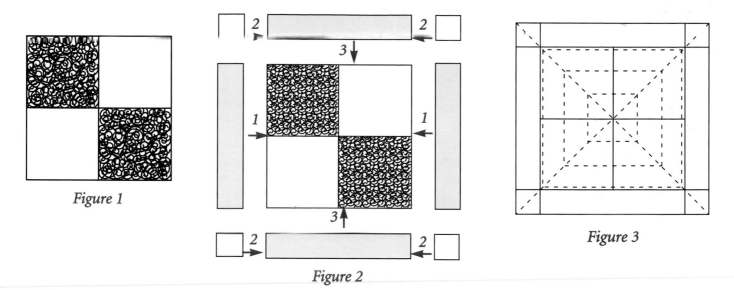

Figure 1

Figure 2

Figure 3

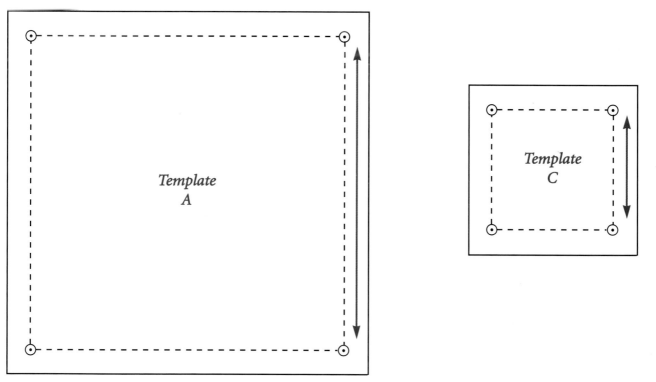

Template
A

Template
C

Template
B

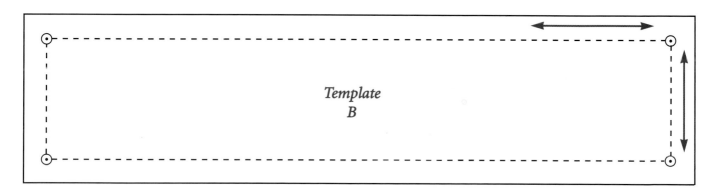

ERNESTINE

(74" x 84")
(Experienced)

Fifty-six "King David's Crown" blocks are straight set and separated by large setting pieces. Similar fabrics are placed in long diagonal rows.

Technique:
Precision hand or machine piecing

Fabrics:
Interesting light and bright '40s prints; red solid or print; dark print; medium blue print

Approximate yardage:
Wide variety of fabrics for the "kites," totaling an estimated 2-1/2 yards
1 yard red and 1/3 yard dark for the center squares
3 yards for the setting pieces and border

Assembly:

1. For each block (Figure 1), mark and cut four kites using Template A. (Note: The small letter "a" is to match the small letter "a" in Template C.) Mark and cut five squares using Template B, four red and one dark print.

2. Precision piece each block as shown in Figure 2. Numbers indicate the piecing sequence, and the arrows indicate suggested a seam pressing direction.

3. Mark and cut the setting pieces using Template C (need forty-eight vertical and forty-nine horizontal; sixteen vertical halves and fourteen horizontal halves)

4. Assemble in rows 1 and 2 as partially shown in Figure 3, seven blocks across and eight blocks down.

5. Add 2-1/2" border, or personal preference.

Quilting:
Optional continuous-line quilting tracks are shown in Figures 4 and 5. The black and blue dotted lines represent vertical tracks and the red and green dotted lines represent horizontal tracks.

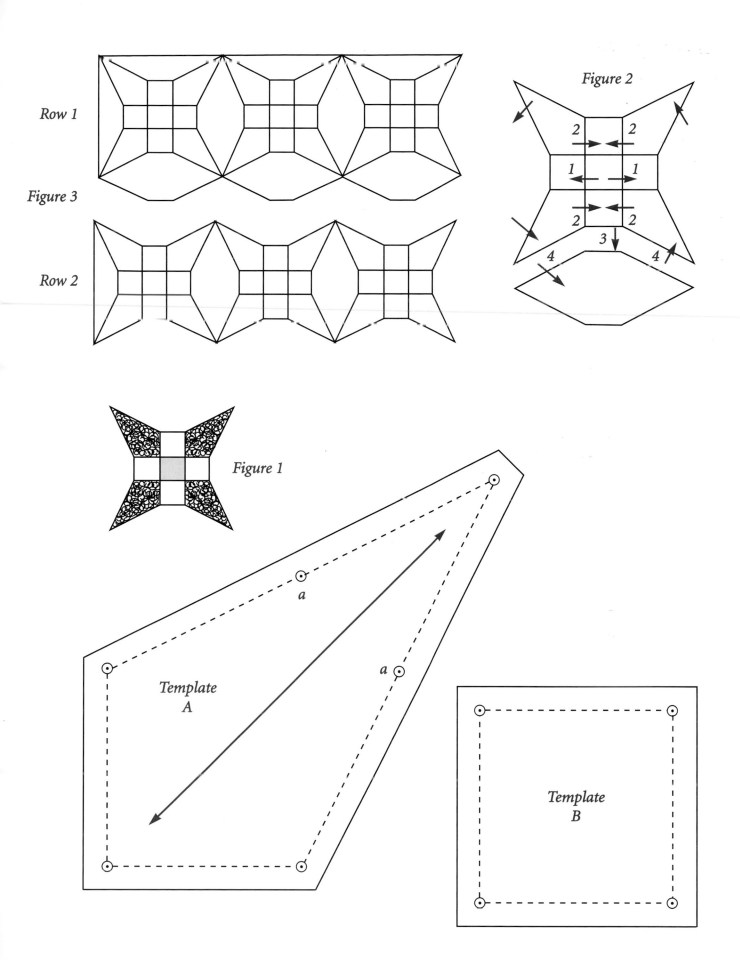

Row 1

Figure 3

Row 2

Figure 2

Figure 1

Template A

Template B

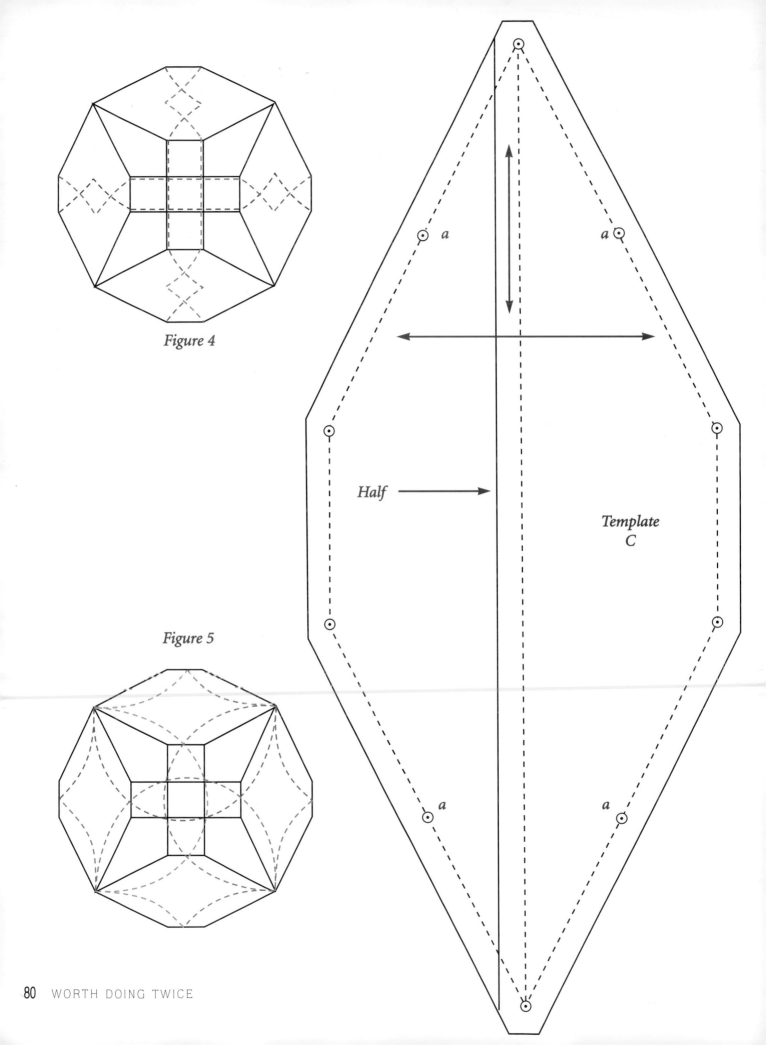

Figure 4

Figure 5

a   *a*

Half →

Template C

a   *a*

FLORENCE

(44" x 52")
(Intermediate)

Cheerful checkerboard basket blocks, made of '20s fabrics, and defying all reasonable rules of straight of grain, are set on point and separated by sashing and posts.

Technique:
Piecing, by hand or machine

Fabrics:
Red print or red/white polka dot for the baskets and posts; bleached or unbleached muslin; striped shirting or pajama-type for the large half-squares; blue print for the sashing and border

Approximate yardage:
1/4 yard red
1/4 yard muslin
1 yard shirting
2 yards blue for the sashing and border

Assembly:

1. *For each block, mark and cut six red squares and four muslin squares using Template A, five small muslin half-squares using Template B, and one large shirting half-square using Template C.*

2. *Assemble each block as shown in Figure 1. Prepare a total of thirty-two blocks.*

3. *Cut the sashing pieces using Template D.*

4. *Assemble the blocks in diagonal rows with sashing between, as begun in Figure 2.*

5. *Add half-posts (Template B) and large fill-in half-squares (Template C) at the ends of the rows where necessary.*

6. *Join the posts (Template A) to the ends of the additional sashing pieces and stitch to the rows of blocks, as shown in Figure 2.*

7. *Add corners (Template E).*

8. *Add 5" border, or personal preference.*

Quilting:
Stitch in the ditch next to all sashing and posts, just inside the border. The dotted lines in Figure 3 represent optional quilting tracks for basket blocks.

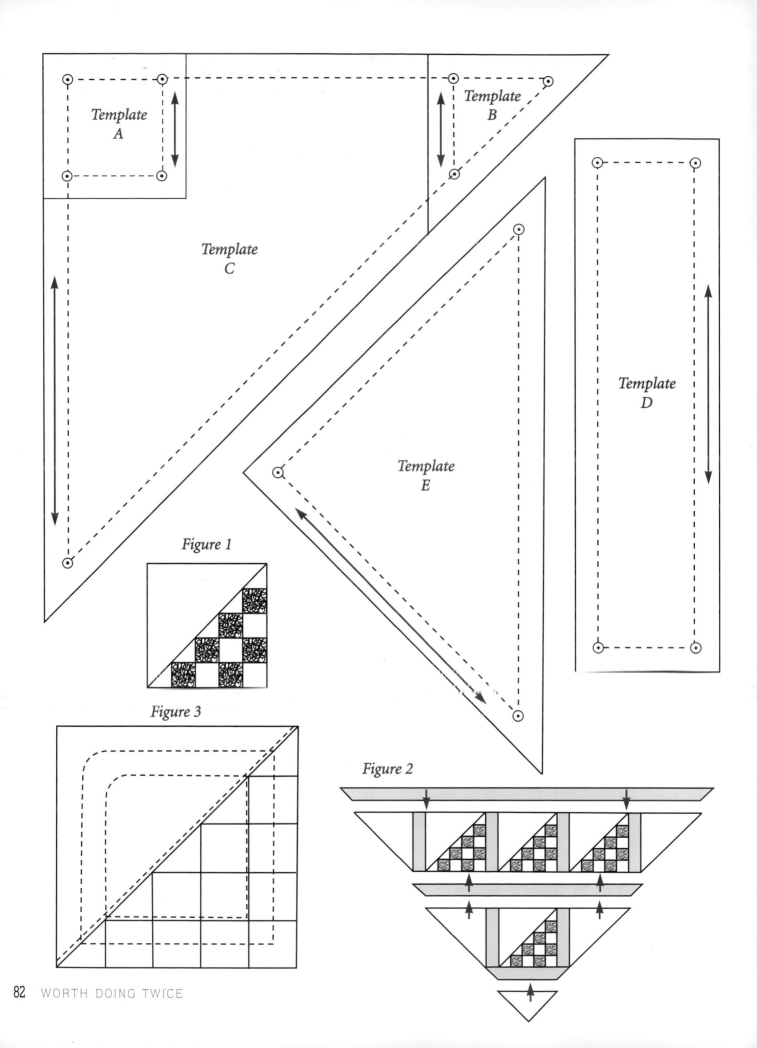

Template
A

Template
B

Template
C

Template
E

Template
D

Figure 1

Figure 3

Figure 2

HARRIET JOSEPHINE

(79″ x 79″)
(Experienced)

Delightful late '40s to early '50s apron fabrics make this a fun and funky "Eight-Pointed Star" variation. Sixteen blocks are straight set and separated by sashing and posts.

Technique:
Precision piecing, by hand or machine

Fabrics:
A wide variety of light/bright and dark/bright prints for the "kites"; bleached muslin for the diamonds and posts; a variety of medium blue for the half-squares; bright print for the sashing and border

Approximate yardage:
Total of 1-3/4 yards light/bright and a total of 1-3/4 yards dark/bright for the kites
Total of 1-1/2 yards medium blue for the half-squares
1 yard muslin for the diamonds and posts
1-1/2 yards bright print for the sashing and border

Assembly:

1. For each 16″ block, mark and cut four light kites and four compatible contrasting kites using Template A.

2. Stitch together, as shown in the center portion of Figure 1. Stitch from circle to circle, leaving all seam allowances unstitched. Press all seams counterclockwise.

3. Mark and cut eight diamonds using Template B.

4. Stitch the diamonds to the edges of the "kites," leaving all seam allowances unstitched. The arrows in Figure 1 indicate the seam pressing direction.

5. Place completed inner portions of all sixteen blocks on a design wall to audition the setting.

6. Mark and cut the half-squares using Template C. Place matching fabrics in the adjoining blocks (see photo of completed quilt, page 31). The letter "a" indicates a construction mark for matching the point of the kite.

7. Stitch the half-squares to the appropriate blocks. Press the seams toward the corners.

8. Mark and cut the sashing pieces and posts using Templates D and E. The letter "a" indicates an additional construction mark.

9. Stitch the sashing between the blocks in each horizontal row. Press the seams toward the sashing.

10. Join the horizontal sashing pieces to the posts and stitch to the rows of blocks.

11. Add the sashing and posts to the outside edge, or add a plain border, as desired. Note: The original top had no border. Leftover fabric has been augmented by reproduction fabric.

Quilting:

Each color indicates an optional individual quilting track. With the exception of the design in the Eight-Pointed Star blocks, all tracks begin and end at an outside edge.

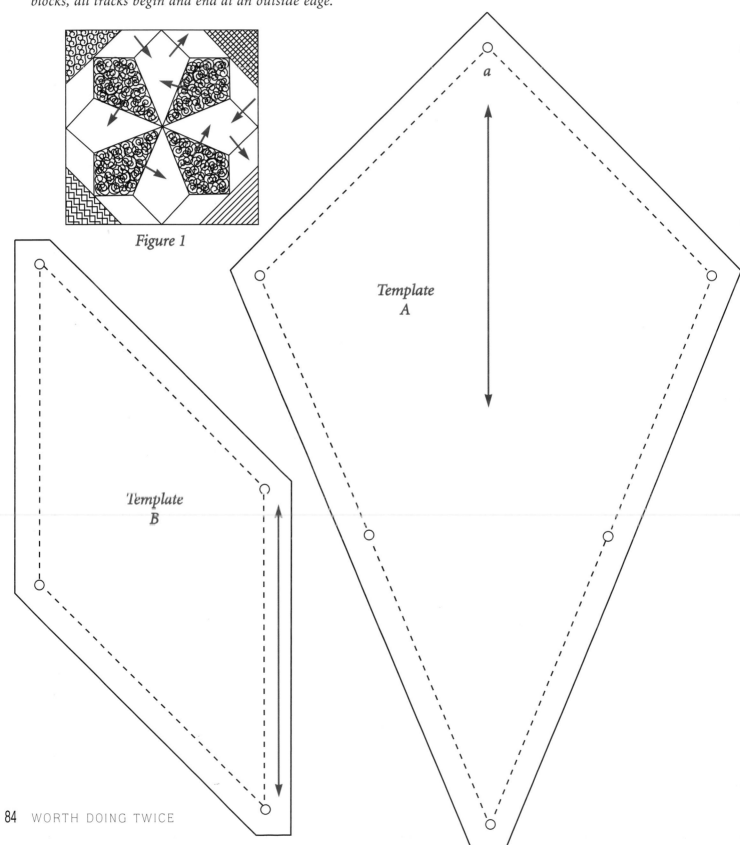

Figure 1

Template A

Template B

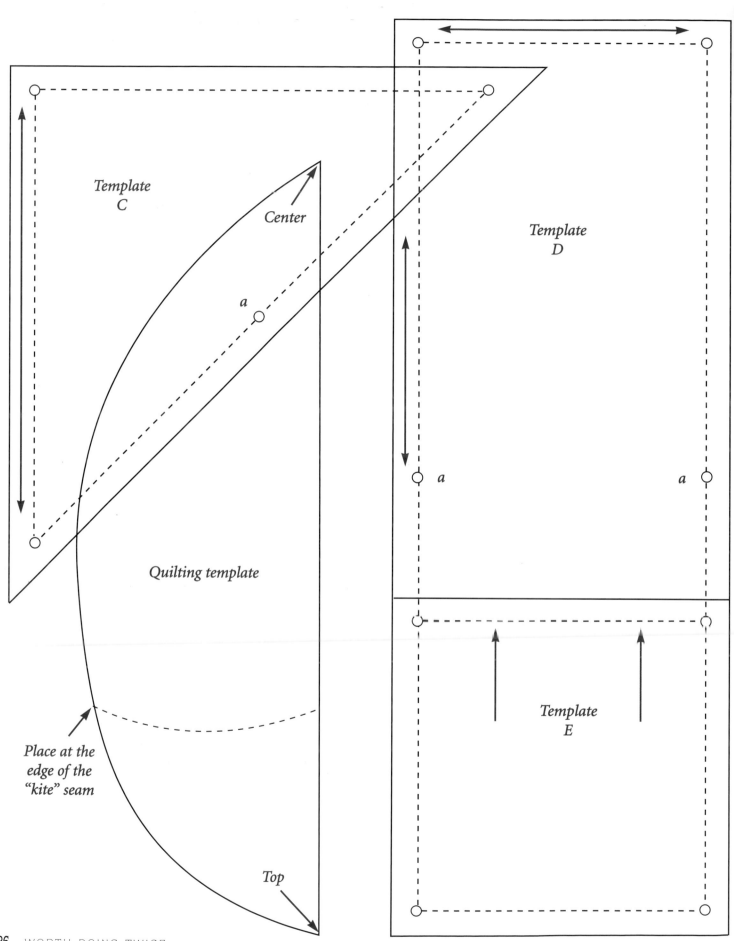

*Template
C*

Center

a

Quilting template

*Place at the
edge of the
"kite" seam*

Top

*Template
D*

a

a

*Template
E*

HAZEL SOPHIA

(62″ x 78″)
(Experienced)

*"Harrison Rose," (Pattern "L"), ©1930 by **Mountain Mist**, is the name of the block used in this quilt. Here, a sawtooth-variation border is substituted, and only the directions for this border are included. Interested quilters may contact the following for pattern information:*

Mountain Mist®
Quilt Center
100 Williams Street
Cincinnati, OH 45215
(513) 948-5307
(800) 345-7150

Techniques:
Appliqué and piecing, by hand or machine

Fabrics:
Muslin; a wide variety of unusual '30s and '40s prints

Assembly:

1. Prepare the appliqué blocks as directed in Pattern "L."

2. Prepare a sawtooth border as partially shown in Figure 1, using Template A. A total of 116 half-square combinations are needed (Figure 2). Note: Both corner half-squares are prints.

3. Attach the completed pieced border to the appliqué section.

4. Add a 6″ plain border, or personal preference.

Quilting:
The dotted lines in Figure 3 represent optional diagonal quilt tracks. Measurements vary, but it is similar to the quilting design shown in the instructions for "Jeannette." Mark 1/2″ increments at the edges of the blocks. Inside increments are 1-7/8″ apart. Or, use quilting designs as suggested in Mountain Mist Pattern "L."

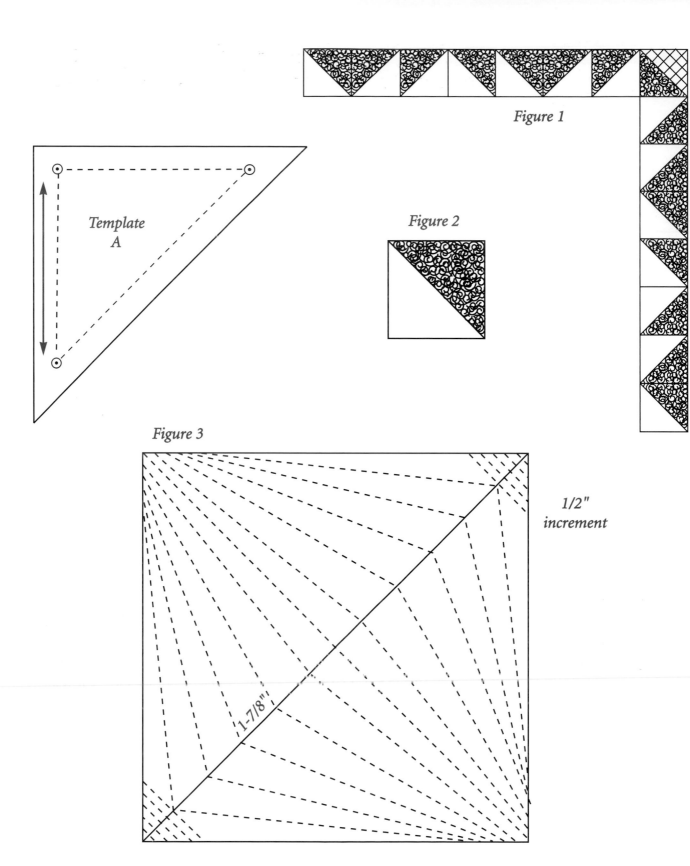

Figure 1

Figure 2

Template
A

Figure 3

1-7/8"

1/2"
increment

IDA CAROLINE

(64" x 64")
(Basic)

*The traditional favorite "Nine-Patch" block is set on point
with alternating plain blocks.*

Technique:
Piecing, by hand or machine

Fabrics:
A wide variety of darks; one light accent color; medium shade for the alternating blocks

Approximate yardage:
1/2 yard dark scraps
1/2 yard light accent color
2 yards for the plain blocks
2 yards for the border

Assembly:
1. *For each "Nine-Patch" block, as shown in Figure 1, cut five dark squares and four light squares, using Template A.*

2. *From the medium fabric, cut thirty-six 6-1/2" squares, straight of grain on point. (Note: The size should match the pieced "Nine-Patch" block.) To make a template for the plain blocks, double Template B.*

3. *From the medium fabric, cut twelve side fill-in triangles using Template B, straight of grain on the long edge; cut twelve top and bottom fill-in triangles using Template B, straight of grain across center, and cut four corners using half of Template B.*

4. *Assemble in diagonal rows as partially shown in Figure 2.*

5. *Add a 2" to 3" border, or personal preference.*

Quilting:
The dotted lines in Figure 2 represent optional continuous-line quilting tracks.

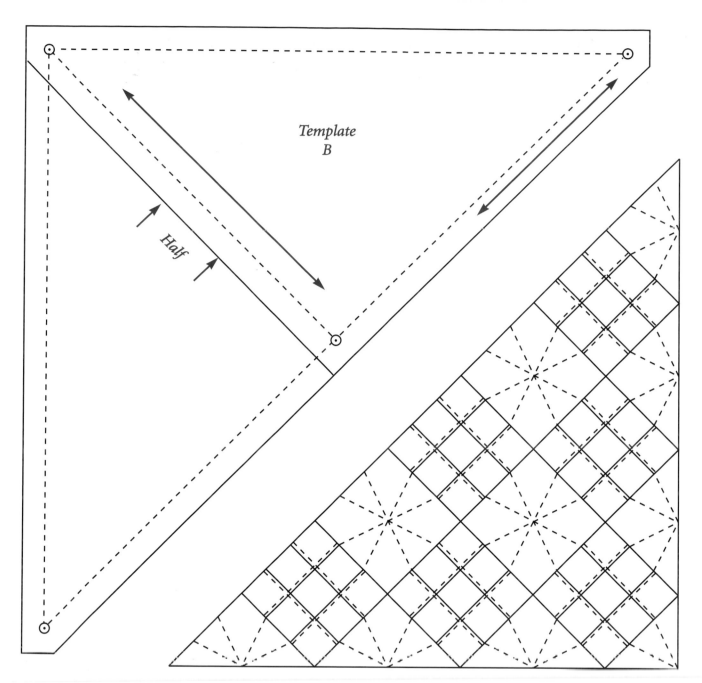

*Template
B*

Half

Figure 2

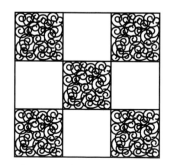

Figure 1

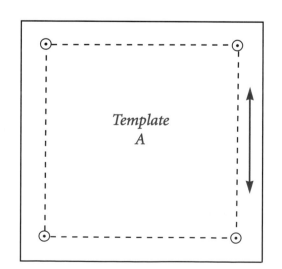

*Template
A*

JEANNETTE

(75″ x 90″)
(Intermediate)

"Thirties-style" baskets of flowers, on-point, alternate with plain blocks, surrounded by a sawtooth inner border.

Techniques:
Appliqué and piecing

Fabrics:
'30s prints; bubble gum pink and Nile green solids; pastel solids; muslin

Approximate yardage:
5 to 6 yards muslin for the blocks and border
1/2 yard for the baskets
1/2 yard for the foliage
Wide variety of prints for the flowers, totaling an estimated 1/2 yard
Small quantities of pastel solid scraps for the flower centers, totaling 1/4 yard
1 yard pink for the sawtooth border

Assembly:

1. *Prepare master templates from the pattern.*

2. *Cut twenty full 12″ blocks from muslin, straight of grain on point.*

3. *Prepare all component parts of the flower baskets and appliqué to the background blocks (see the pattern).*

4. *Carefully trim each block to measure exactly 11″ square (10-1/2″ finished).*

5. *From muslin, cut twelve plain 11″ squares on point.*

6. *From muslin, cut fourteen half-squares.* **Important:** *Be sure to add a 1/4″ seam allowance to the long diagonal edge.*

7. *Also from muslin, cut four quarter-squares for the corners.* **Important:** *Be sure to add a 1/4″ seam allowance.*

8. *Assemble in diagonal rows, alternating appliquéd blocks and plain blocks. Add fill-in triangles and corners to the ends of the rows. The piece will measure approximately 59-1/2″ x 74-1/2″.*

9. *For the sawtooth border, prepare 148 half-square units as shown in Figure 1, using Template A.*

10. *Add the completed sawtooth border to the appliquéd top.*

11. Add a 5-1/2″ plain border, or personal preference.

Quilting:

*The dotted lines in **Figure 2** indicate optional diagonal continuous-line quilting tracks.*

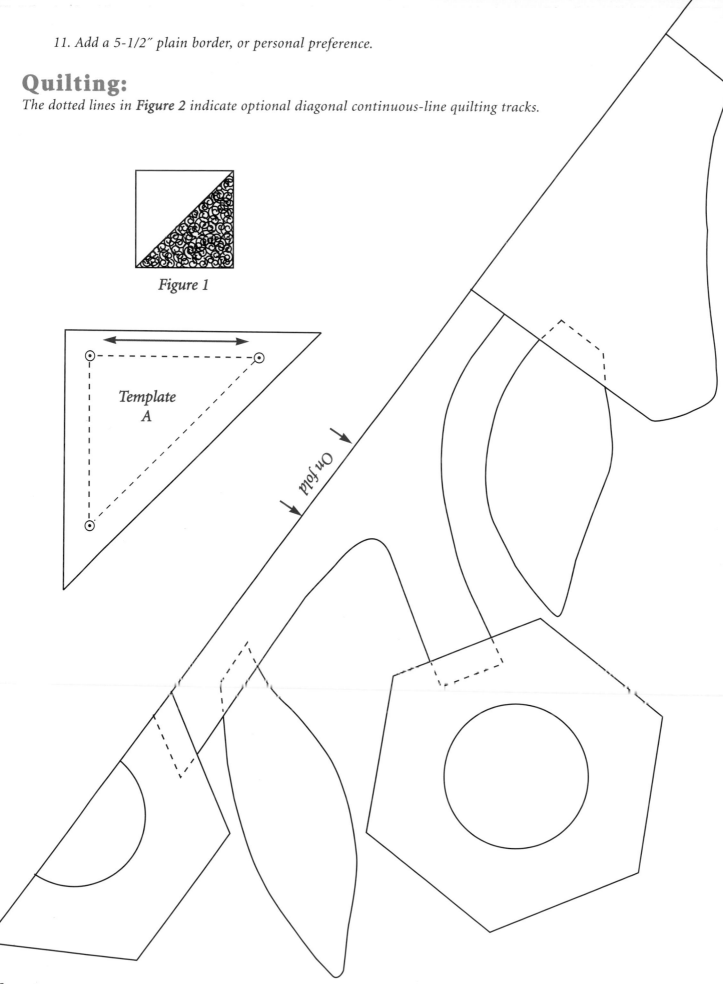

Figure 1

Template
A

On fold

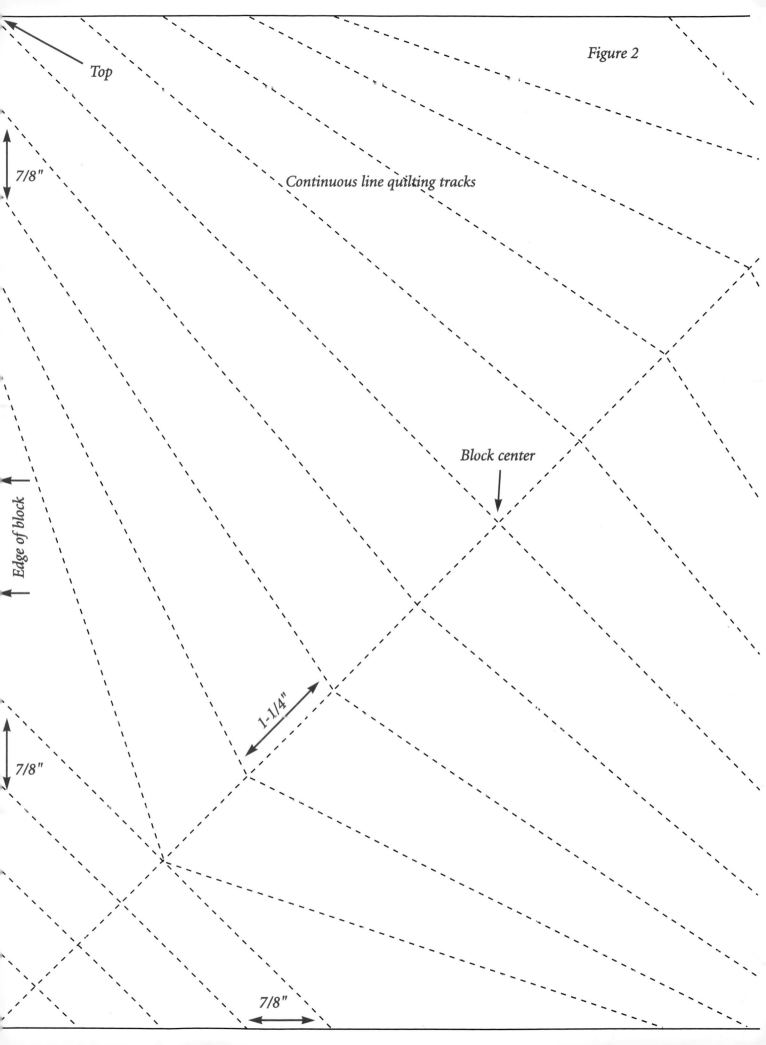

Top

Figure 2

7/8"

Continuous line quilting tracks

Edge of block

Block center

1-1/4"

7/8"

7/8"

JENNY DELL

(61″ x 61″)
(Intermediate)

An unusual setting of an all-time favorite block, "Bow Tie,"
or "Necktie," features four small blocks separated by sashing.

Technique:
Piecing, by hand or machine

Fabrics:
A wide variety of light and dark scraps for the "bow ties"; an accent color for the sashing within the blocks; medium color for the alternating plain blocks; compatible fabric for the border

Approximate yardage:
1/3 yard light and 1/3 yard dark for the blocks
5/8 yard for the sashing
1-1/2 yards for the plain blocks and inner border
1-3/4 yards for the outer border (this may be pieced, requiring less yardage)

Assembly:
1. For each 4″ (finished) block (Figure 1), cut two light and two dark pieces using Template A. Cut one dark using Template B.

2. Assemble as indicated in Figure 2. Numbers indicate the piecing sequence. Press the seams toward the "knot."

3. Prepare four segments for each full block.

4. To complete the block, as shown in Figure 3, cut one sashing piece using Template C and two sashing pieces using Template D. Note: The lower-case letters indicate construction points that match the bow tie and sashing.

5. From plain fabric, cut nine large alternating squares, straight of grain on point, the exact size of the pieced block.

6. From plain fabric, cut side fill-in triangles, with the triangle's long edges on straight of grain, and the triangle's long edges on cross grain for top and bottom fill-in triangles. Also, cut four corner triangles.

7. Place the pieced blocks on a design wall, on point. Fill in with plain blocks and triangles as shown in Figure 4.

9. Assemble in diagonal rows.

10. Add a 2″ inner border and a 3-1/2″ outer border, or personal preference.

Quilting:

*The dotted lines in **Figure 4** represent optional, continuous-line quilting tracks, for the plain blocks. All seams in the pieced blocks may be quilted in the ditch.*

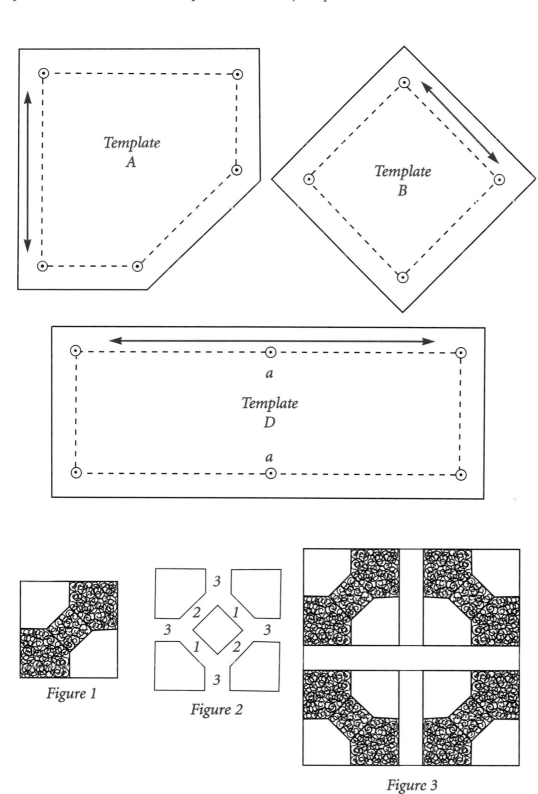

Template A

Template B

Template D

a

a

Figure 1

Figure 2

Figure 3

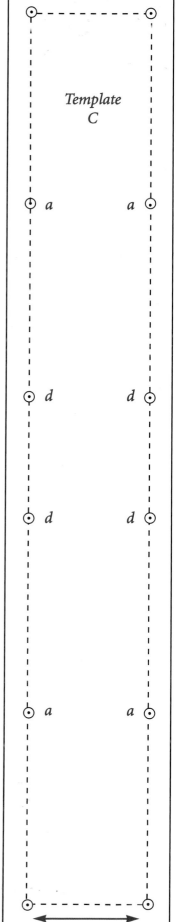

Template C

a   a

d   d

d   d

a   a

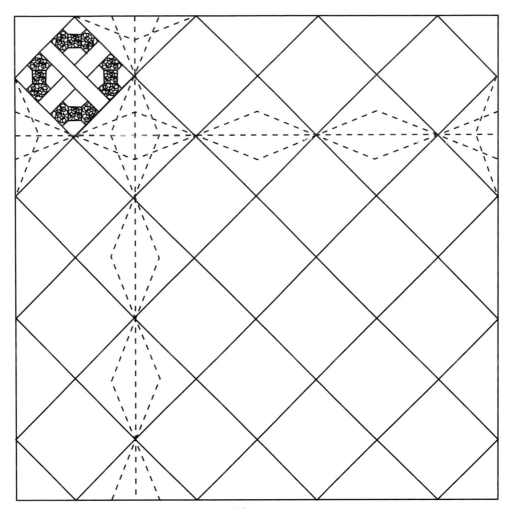

Figure 4

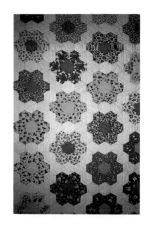

JESSIE
(62″ x 85″)
(Intermediate)

A medallion arrangement of honeycombs, a variation of "Grandmother's Flower Garden," is set apart by a muslin "path" and appliquéd to an inner border.

Techniques:
English piecing and appliqué

Fabrics:
A wide variety of '30s prints; muslin; solids; bubble gum pink

Approximate yardage:
Large quantity of scraps, or an estimated ten to twelve "fat quarters" for the honeycomb units
Variety of solid colors, for the honeycomb centers, totaling 1/2 yard
3 yards muslin for the "paths" and inner border
2-1/2 yards pink for the outer border

Assembly:

1. Make a permanent master template, using Template A.

2. For each honeycomb unit, cut seven paper patterns, using the master template.

3. Pin the paper patterns to the wrong side of the fabric and cut, adding a 1/4″ seam allowance.

4. Fold seam allowances over the edges of the papers and baste.

5. Assemble each honeycomb unit as shown in Figure 1, using the English piecing method. Prepare a total of 127 full units and sixteen partial units, as shown in Figure 2.

6. Beginning in the center, stitch the honeycomb units together, inserting muslin hexagons between each unit. Complete four full concentric "rounds."

7. Begin adding partial units at the edge to maintain a rectangular shape (refer to the photo of full quilt, page 41).

8. Add two more rows of honeycomb units at the top and bottom.

9. Remove the papers from the hexagons.

10. Cut two 2″ strips of muslin, 3″ to 4″ longer than the side measurement. Cut two 2-1/4″ strips of muslin, slightly longer than measurement of the top or bottom.

11. Tape the muslin strips to a large, flat surface. Pin and baste the entire top to the muslin strips.

12. Fold the muslin strips back at the corners. Finger crease and appliqué closed. Trim away excess muslin.

13. Hand appliqué all hexagon edges to the muslin.

14. Add a 3″ border, or personal preference.

Quilting:

The blue, green, and black (gold) dotted lines in Figure 3 represent optional, diagonal continuous-line quilting tracks, and the red dotted lines represent horizontal tracks.

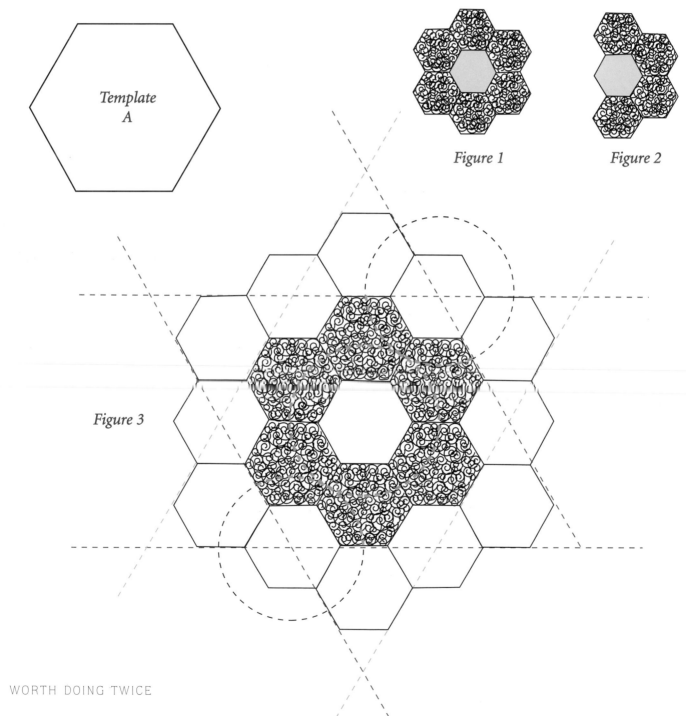

Template
A

Figure 1

Figure 2

Figure 3

KIRTLEY

(85″ x 85″)
(Experienced)

"St. Andrew's Cross" blocks are set on point in a zigzag strip-pie-style. Forty-six full blocks and six half blocks are used.

Technique:
Piecing, by hand or machine

Fabrics:
Bright yellow, dark green, and bright red prints; regularly patterned bright blue print

Approximate yardage:
1/4 yard dark green for the block centers
1-1/2 yard red for the blocks
2 yards yellow for the blocks and inner border
5 yards bright blue for the large setting triangles and outer border

Assembly:

1. For each full block (*Figure 1*), mark and cut four triangles, using Template A, four pieces, using Template B, and one small square, using Template C.

2. Assemble as shown in *Figure 1*. Prepare forty-six full blocks.

3. For each half block (*Figure 2*), mark and cut two triangles, using Template A, one piece, using Template B, two pieces, using half of Template B, and one half of Template C. Prepare six.

4. For the large setting triangles, use Template D. Cut ninety.

5. For the corners and small setting triangles, use half of Template D. Cut sixteen.

6. Assemble in long rows, as partially indicated in *Figure 3*.

7. Add a 1-1/2″ inner border and a 5″ outer border, or personal preference.

Quilting:
*The dotted lines in *Figure 4* represent optional quilting tracks.*

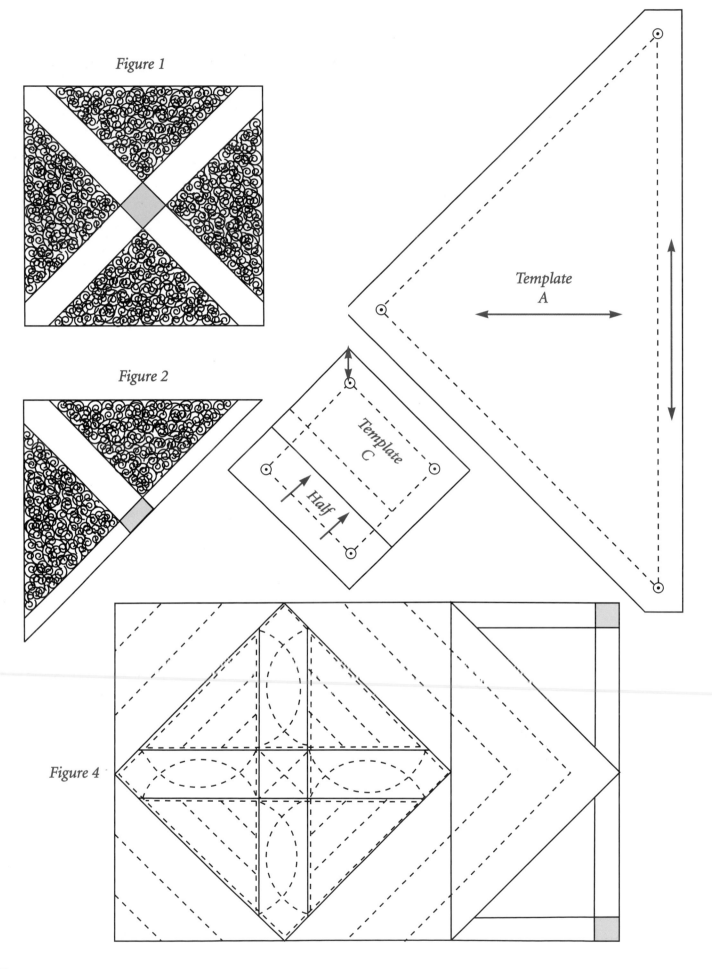

Figure 1

Figure 2

Template
A

Template
C

Half

Figure 4

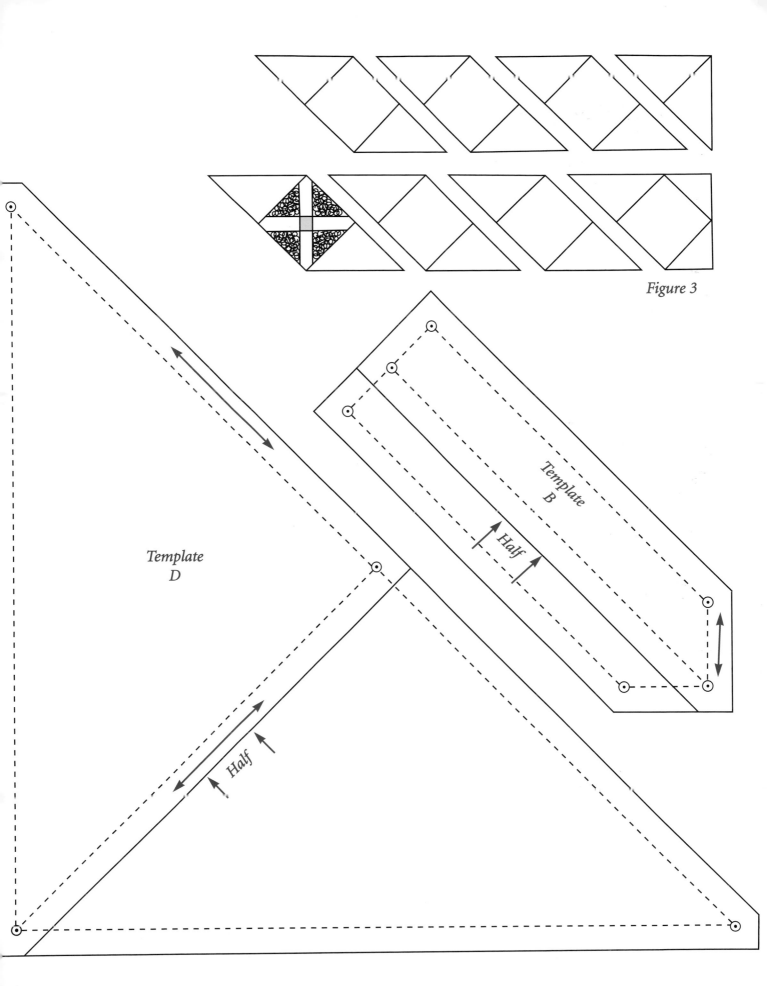

Figure 3

Template
D

Template
B

Half

Half

NELLIE

(52″ x 52″)
(Intermediate)

Embroidered blocks from "Cute Little Quilts for the Children," designed by Signe I. Pinch, owner of Rainbow Quilts Company, are straight set and sashed. The stamped blocks were readily available from the late 1920s until the 1980s. The search for the current copyright holder has been unsuccessful.

Techniques:
Embroidery and piecing, by hand or machine

Fabrics:
White or bleached muslin for blocks, or purchase completed blocks; '30s green for sashing and border

Approximate yardage:
1-1/4 yards white or bleached muslin
3 yards green for the sashing, border, and optional prairie points

Assembly:
1. *Cut twenty-five 9″ squares.*

2. *Seek '30s-style embroidery designs. Enlarge or reduce, as necessary, to fit 7-1/2″ (finished) squares.*

3. *Embroider and embellish the blocks, as desired.*

4. *Measure and trim the completed blocks to equal 8″ squares (7-1/2″ finished).*

5. *Stitch 3″ x 8″ sashing between the blocks, in rows of five.*

6. *Stitch 3″ sashing between the rows, or add 3″ posts between each sashing piece for strength and alignment.*

7. *Optional: Add twenty-nine prairie points (prepared from 2″ squares) to each side.*

Quilting:
The dotted lines in Figure 1 represent optional quilting tracks. Quilt in the ditch at the edge of each block. Nine "ties," front to back, are evenly spaced in each block.

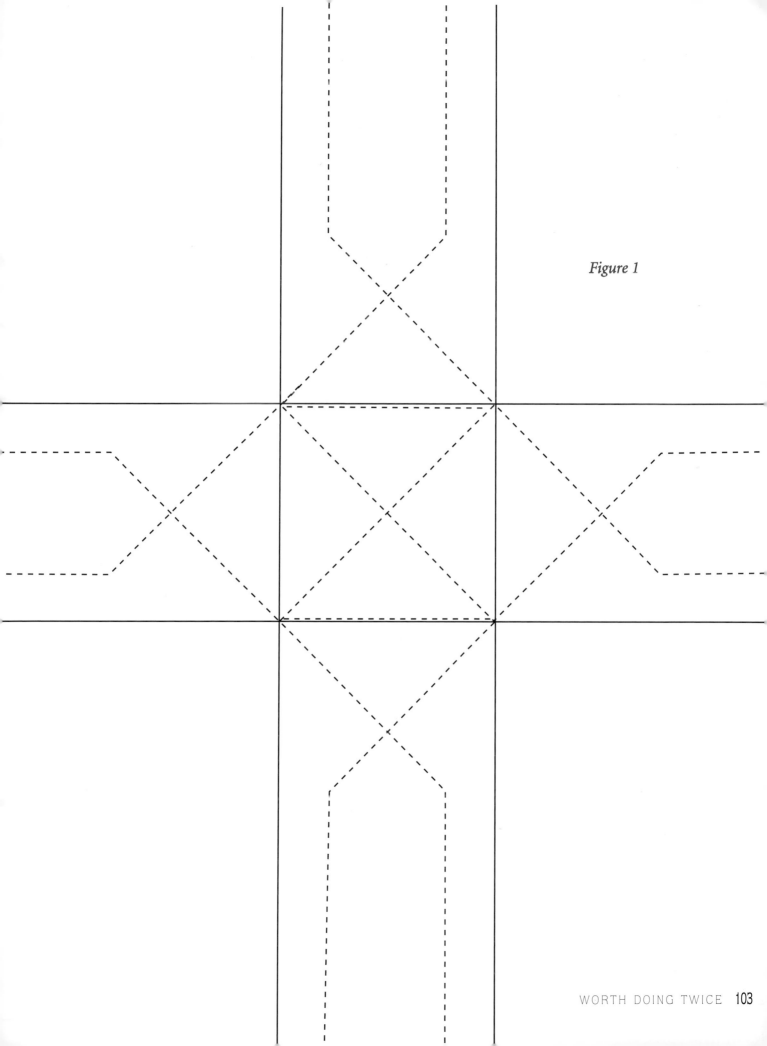

Figure 1

PRISCILLA

(47" x 61")
(Experienced)

"Milky Way," a hexagon block pattern, is set in four vertical rows of nine and three vertical rows of eight.

Technique:
Machine paper/foundation piecing

Fabrics:
Soft pastel '20s and '30s style prints

Approximate yardage:
*Wide variety of leftovers and scraps totaling an **estimated** 1/2 yard*
1 yard print for the inner border (requires piecing) and blocks
2-1/2 yards muslin for the blocks, inner, and outer border

Assembly:
1. *Prepare paper foundation patterns, using the master pattern (prepare sixty). **Important:** Be sure to leave a 1/4" seam allowance beyond the outside edge.*

2. *Using Template A, cut one muslin and three print triangles. Strips are cut 1-1/4".*

3. *Pin the muslin triangle in the center of the paper foundation pattern. Add pieces following Figure 1, working from the center out.*

4. *Prepare a total of sixty completed hexagon units as shown in Figure 1*

5. *Place units on a design wall to audition the setting (see Figure 2). Place the point of the light center triangles **up** in all rows except as indicated by **down** arrows.*

6. *For side fill-in segments, use Template B. Corner segments are half of Template B.*

7. *For the top and bottom fill-in segments, use Template C.*

8. *Precision stitch all units together.*

9. *Add a 1-3/4" inner muslin border, 1-1/4" print border, and a 3-1/2" outer muslin border, or personal preference.*

10. *Remove the foundation papers.*

Quilting:

The dotted lines on the master pattern represent optional continuous-line diagonal and vertical tracks. Note: Shallow curves are made using a radius of approximately 5-1/2″; other curves are made using a 6″ protractor.

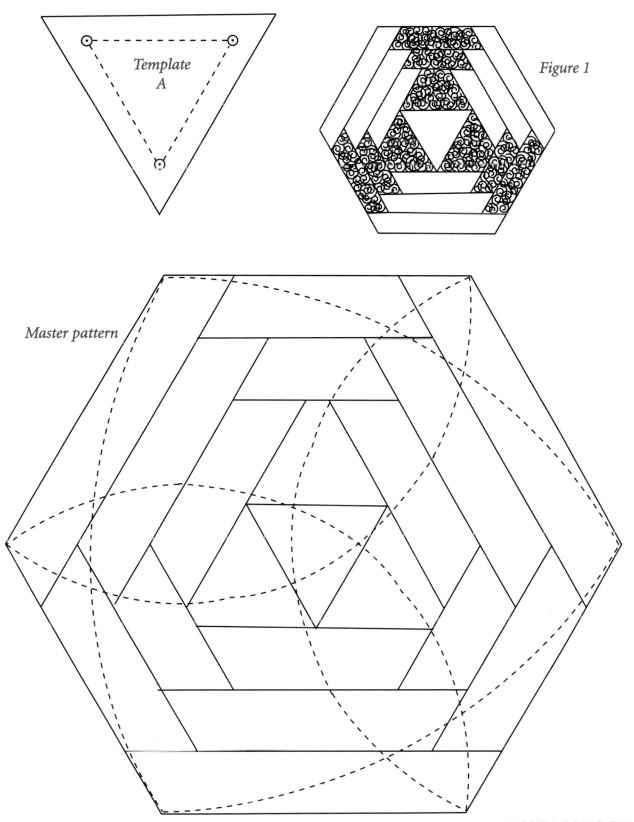

Template A

Figure 1

Master pattern

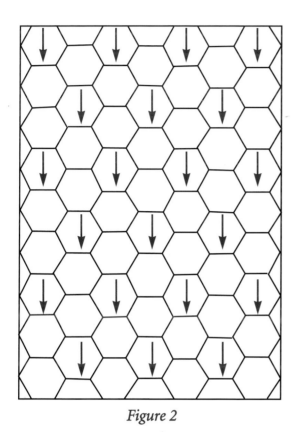

Figure 2

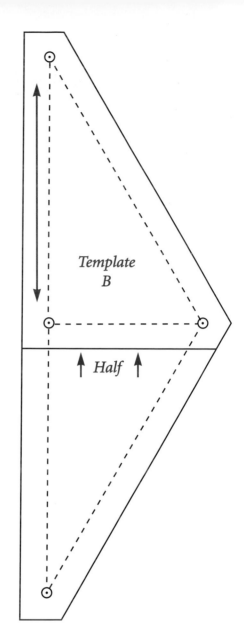

*Template
B*

Half

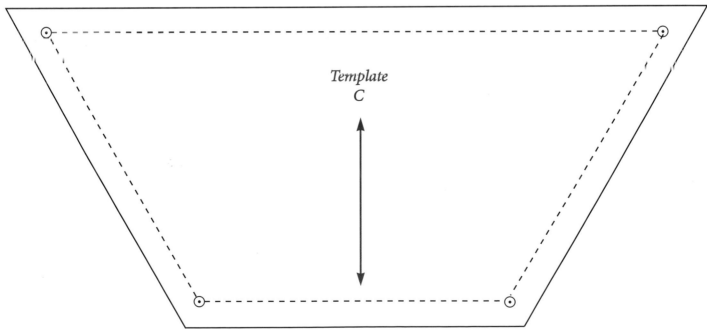

*Template
C*

SARAH ABIGAIL
(62" x 75")
(Intermediate)

Light and dark half-square blocks make up this asymmetrical "Barn Raising" design. It is straight set in sixteen rows of thirteen blocks each. The size may easily be altered; increase or decrease the yardage as necessary.

Technique:
Piecing, by hand or machine

Fabrics:
A wide variety of light and dark scraps and some accent colors (be sure to vary the intensity of the lights and darks)

Approximate yardage:
Total of 2 yards light scraps
Total of 2 yards dark scraps
Accent scraps
2-1/2 yards for the border (this may be pieced, requiring less yardage)

Assembly:
1. Mark and cut 208 light half-squares and 208 dark half-squares using Template A.

2. Stitch the half-squares together in light and dark pairs as shown in Figure 1. Note: For this project, the lightest "lights" were paired with the lightest "darks" and the darkest "lights" were paired with the darkest "darks" (see photo of completed quilt, page 49).

3. Audition the blocks on a design wall and stitch together, continuing to alternate dark and light rows as begun in Figure 2.

4. Add a 2" to 3" border, or personal preference.

Quilting:
The red, green, and blue dotted lines in Figure 3 represent optional quilting tracks. Shallow curves and zigzag lines are suggested for light areas and zigzags in the dark areas.

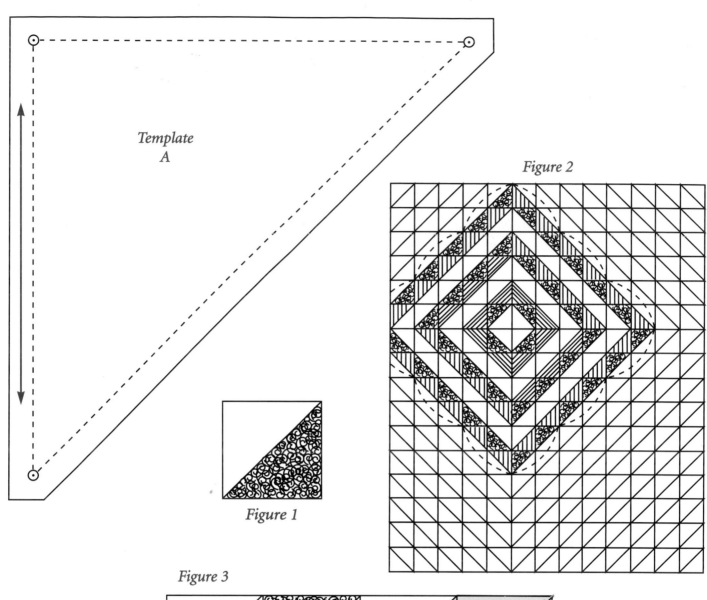

Template
A

Figure 2

Figure 1

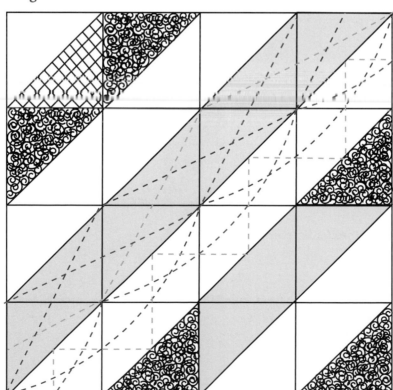

Figure 3

SUSIE BELL

(34-1/2" x 50")
(Intermediate)

Simple animal shapes make a delightful crib quilt. The pattern source for these '30s animals is unknown. Patterns based on the original animals are not included because many of them have lost their original appendages and embroidery details over the years, especially the cow.

Techniques:
Appliqué and piecing, by hand or machine

Fabrics:
A variety of '30s prints for motifs; muslin, bleached or unbleached, for the blocks; medium-colored print for the sashing and border

Approximate yardage:
Assorted scraps for the appliqués
1-1/4 yards for the background squares
1-1/4 yards medium for the sashing and border (this may be pieced, requiring less yardage)

Assembly:

1. *Select simple motifs from coloring books, magazines, greeting cards, or children's drawings. Use a copier to reduce or enlarge the designs.*

2. *Using your favorite method, transfer the motifs to fabric and appliqué to 7-1/2" background squares. Prepare twenty-four.*

3. *Embellish and embroider as desired. Note: It was popular in the 1930s to use black embroidery cotton and a separated blanket stitch to secure each shape. The edges were frequently unturned.*

4. *Cut the sashing strips 2" x 7-1/2".*

5. *Sew the sashing between the blocks in rows of four.*

6. *Stitch 2" strips between each row, using the exact measurement of the completed rows.*

7. *Add a 2" border, or personal preference.*

Quilting:
For optional quilting tracks, quilt in all ditches. Quilting pattern 1 may be used in each block. The shape is four hearts, representing the four generations of women who have used this quilt. Use quilting pattern 2, point to point, in the sashing and border. (The original quilt was tied.)

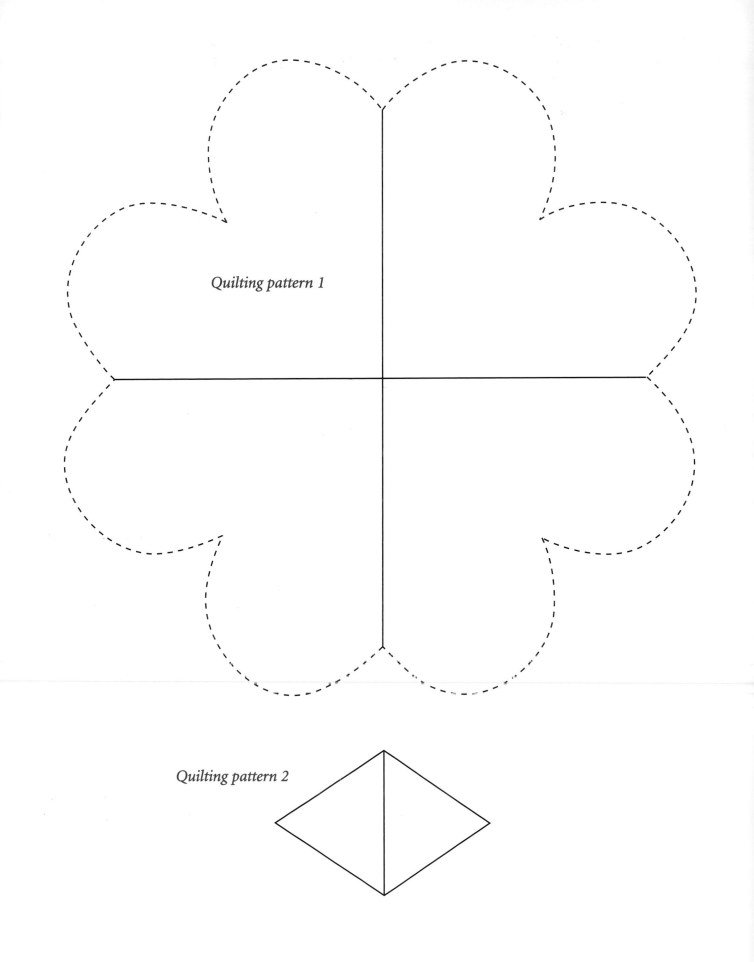

Quilting pattern 1

Quilting pattern 2

THELMA

(56" x 56")
(Intermediate)

A traditional favorite, the "Thousand Pyramids" design features a single shape, a tessellation. Dark triangles point up, and light triangles point down, to create the illusion, as the title suggests.

Technique:

Piecing, by hand or machine

Fabrics:

A wide variety of light and dark colors; compatible fabric for the border. Be sure to vary the color intensities

Approximate yardage:

Total of 1 yard scraps for the light triangles
Total of 1 yard scraps for the dark triangles
2 yards for the border and side fill-in shapes

Assembly:

1. Using Template A, cut eighty light triangles and eighty dark triangles (this allows a few more than actually needed).

2. Place the triangles on a design wall, beginning with the nine darkest darks at the bottom. Fill in the lights. Continue, alternating darks and lights as begun in Figure 1. Audition as desired. (The completed quilt has nine rows, see page 53.)

3. Mark and cut the side fill-in pieces from the border fabric, using Templates B and C.

4. Assemble in diagonal rows.

5. Add a 3" border, or personal preference.

Quilting:

Stitch all long diagonal tracks in the ditch. For horizontal tracks in light areas, use quilting Template 1 (6" protractor), and for diagonal tracks in light areas, use quilting Template 2 (8" protractor). For horizontal tracks in dark areas, use quilting Templates 3 and 4.

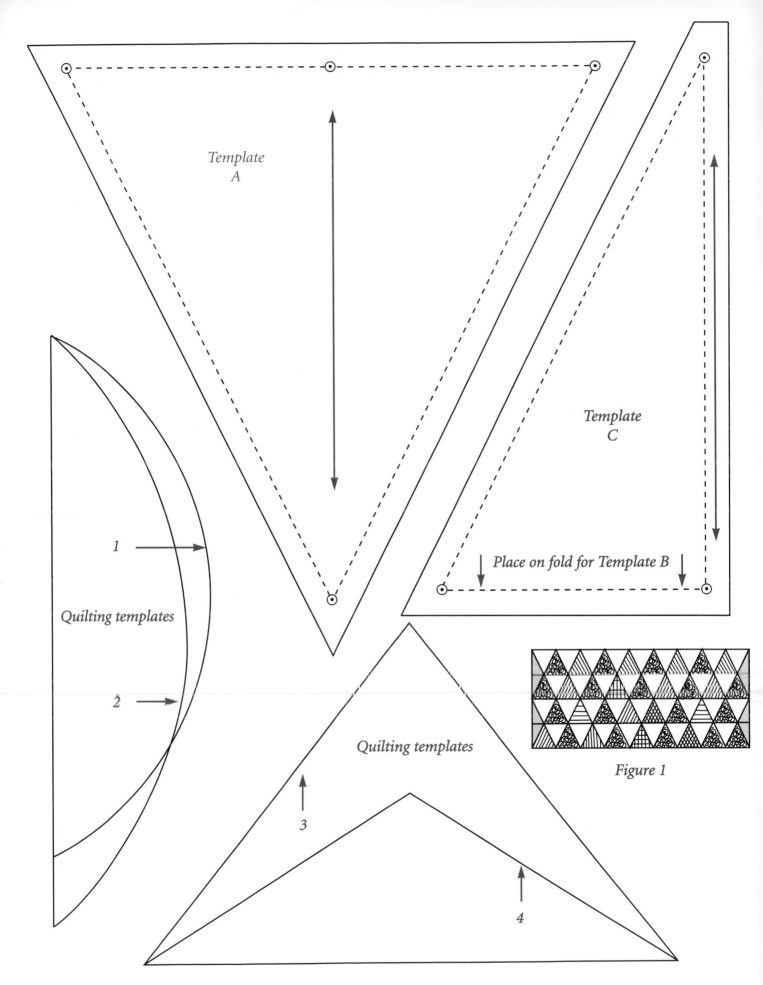

Template
A

Template
C

Place on fold for Template B

1

Quilting templates

2

Quilting templates

3

4

Figure 1

VIDA

(64″ x 54″)
(Basic)

*A simple "Four Patch" block is vertically placed edge to edge
in a strippie setting.*

Technique:
Piecing, by hand or machine

Fabrics:
*A wide variety of light, medium, and dark scraps for the four-patch units; dark accent color for the long strips and
inner border; interesting compatible striped fabric for the outer border*

Approximate yardage:
*Light, medium, and dark scraps totaling 2 yards
2 yards dark for the strips and inner border
2 yards striped fabric for the outer border*

Assembly:

1. *For each block, cut two light 3″ squares and two dark/medium 3″ squares, or use Template A.*

2. *Assemble as shown in* Figure 1. *Prepare forty-eight units (5″ finished).*

3. *Stitch eight units together in vertical rows. Prepare six rows.*

4. *Accurately measure the length of the pieced four-patch strips and cut five 4-1/4″ strips using this measurement.*

5. *Stitch long strips between each pieced strip, as partially shown in* Figure 2.

6. *Add a 2-1/2″ inner border and a 5″ outer border, or personal preference.*

Quilting:
The dotted lines in Figure 2 *indicate optional quilting tracks. A quilting template may be used in plain strips.
Overlap as shown.*

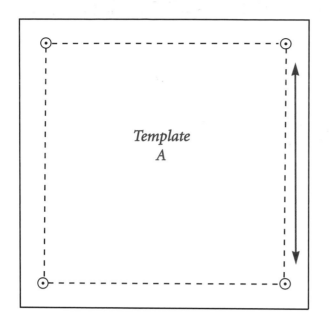

Template A

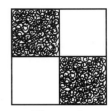

Figure 1

Figure 2

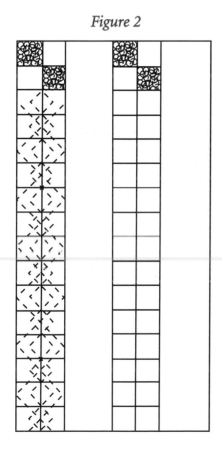

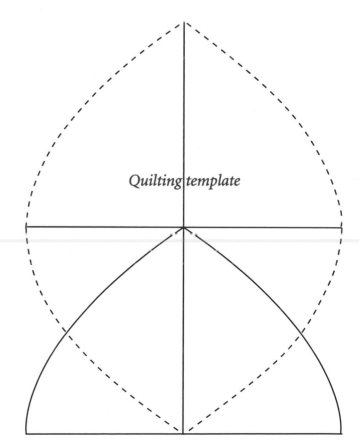

Quilting template

ZAMA BELLE

(39" x 48")
(Experienced)

"Colonial Basket" blocks, a favorite pattern of the late 1800s, are set, four by six, on point with alternating plain blocks.

Techniques:
Appliqué and piecing, by hand or machine

Fabrics:
Two bright pinks, bright yellow, and dark green small prints

Approximate yardage:
3/4 yard dark green, 1/2 yard yellow, 1/4 yard pink for the baskets
2 yards pink for the plain blocks and border

Assembly:

1. *For each block (Figure 1), mark and cut one dark triangle using Template A.*

2. *Prepare the "handle" using the pattern as shown on Template A. Appliqué in place.*

3. *To complete each pieced block, mark and cut two dark rectangles using Template B, one dark triangle using Template C, eleven small yellow triangles using Template D, five pink triangles using Template D, and one pink square using Template E.*

4. *Assemble in segments as suggested in Figure 2. Prepare twenty pieced and appliquéd blocks.*

5. *Cut twelve plain blocks, straight of grain on point, to match the size of the pieced blocks.*

6. *Stitch in diagonal rows, adding the side setting triangles, Template F, at the ends of the rows. The corner triangle is half of Template F.*

7. *Add a 2" border, or personal preference.*

Quilting:
The dotted lines in Figure 3 represent optional quilting tracks. Long diagonal tracks are quilted in the ditch.

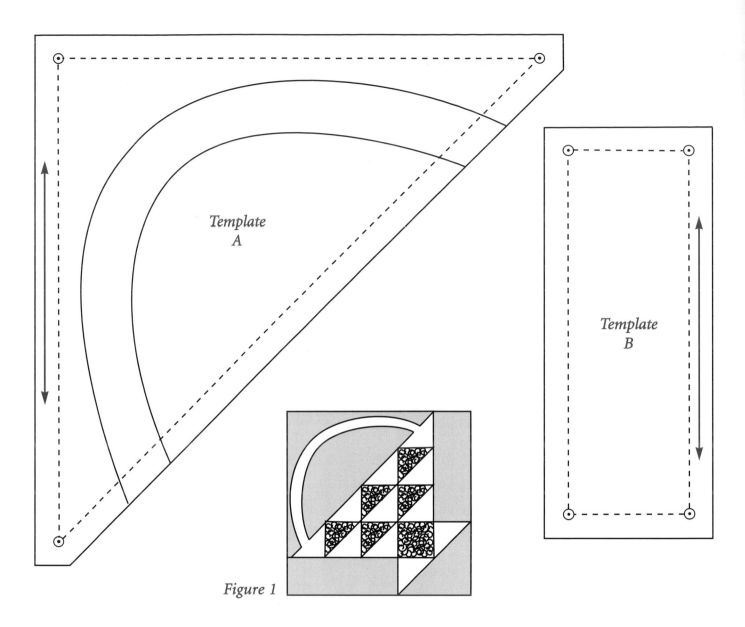

Template
A

Template
B

Figure 1

Figure 2

Figure 3

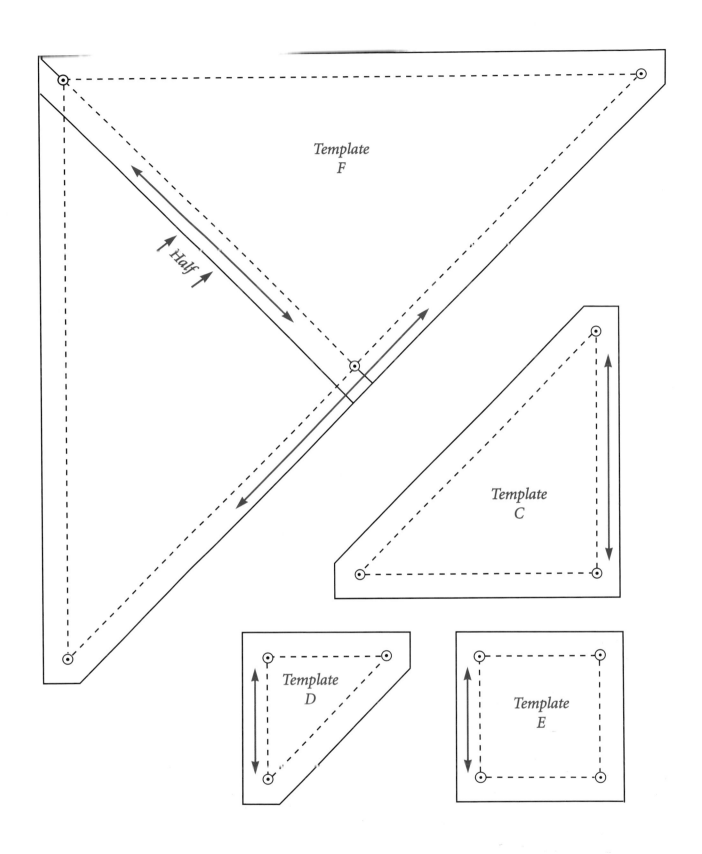

Template
F

Half

Template
C

Template
D

Template
E

ADDENDUM

All of the quilts are named after Jeannette's relatives or friends.

Bertha Robertson Macdonald Pingree, dec. 1976, "Aunt"/Friend

Blanche (Jessie) Tousley Randall, 1882–1957, Aunt (Sister of Jeannette's father, Charles Vernon Tousley, 1899–1992)

Elizabeth Florence Denver Tousley, Keene, NH (Jeannette's Mother)

Elsie Mildred Othick Sibley Bowker, 1887–1976, Great Aunt (Mother's Aunt)

Ernestine Haliburton Macdonald, Lynnfield, MA, "Aunt"/Friend

Florence Wallace Morse, 1902–1987, "Aunt"/Friend

Harriet Josephine Mead Raymond, Medford, NJ, Friend

Hazel Sophia Sheldon Tousley, 1896–1943, Aunt (Sister-in-law of Charles V. Tousley)

Ida Caroline Lawson Tousley, 1864–1906, Paternal Grandmother (Mother of Charles V. Tousley)

Jeannette Gail Tousley Muir, Moorestown, NJ (co-author)

Jenny Dell Othick Taylor, 1863–?, Great Aunt (Mother's Aunt)

Jessie Cundy MacDonald, 1922–1988, Friend

Kirtley Edwards Tate Bishop, Denton, TX, "Aunt"/Friend

Nellie Melendy Tousley, 1870–1950, Step-Grandmother

Priscilla Ilsley Minott, 1903–1976, "Aunt"/Friend

Sarah Abigail Carpenter Othick, 1844–1919, Great Grandmother (Mother's Grandmother)

Susie Bell Othick Denver, 1868–1936, Grandmother (Mother's Mother)

Thelma Kirch Barr, Woodbridge, VA, Friend

Vida Forgey, 1903–1992, "Aunt"/Friend

Zama Belle Austin Tousley, West Hartford, CT; N. Ferrisburg, VT (Wife of first cousin Orwell Charles Tousley)

RESOURCE LIST

American Quilter's Society
P.O. Box 3290
Paducah, KY 42002-3290
(Certified appraisers, books)

Auntie Em's Attic, Emily Hooper
103 S. Martin
Osage City, KS 66523
(785) 528-4771
(Antique quilts and tops)

Cindy's Quilts
P.O. Box 1212
Clinton, OK 73601
(Antique quilts and tops)

Clotilde Inc.
B 3000
Louisiana, MO 63353-3000
(800) 772-2891 (Credit card orders), (800) 863-3191 (Fax orders), (800) 545-4002 (Customer service), www.clotilde.com (Mail order)

Connecting Threads
P.O. Box 8940
Vancouver, WA 98668-8940
(800) 574-6454 (Credit card orders), (360) 260-8877 (Fax orders), (800) 574-6454 (Customer service)
(Mail order)

Crazy Ladies & Friends
1606 Santa Monica Blvd.
Santa Monica, CA 90404
(1″ brass pins and other mail order)

Diane Reese
4 Powhatan Rd.
Pepperill, MA 01463
(Antique quilts and tops)

Fairfield Processing Corp.
P.O. Box 1157
Danbury, CT 06810
(Batting)

Julia Bright Antiques
1349 West Wood St.
Decatur, IL 62522
(Antique quilts and tops)

Keepsake Quilting
Rt. 25B, P.O. Box 1618
Centre Harbor, NH 03226-1618
(Mail order)

Kirk Collection
1513 Military Ave.
Omaha, NE 68111
(Antique fabrics, quilts, and tops)

Merikay Waldvogel
1501 Whitower Rd.
Knoxville, TN 37919
(Author, curator, lecturer)

Mountain Mist Quilt Center
The Stearns Technical Textiles Co.
100 Williams St.
Cincinnati, OH 45215-4683
(Batting and patterns)

Nancy's Notions
P.O. Box 683
Beaver Dam, WI 53916-0683
(Mail order)

Nasco-Fort Atkinson
901 Janesville Ave.
Fort Atkinson, WI 53538-0901
(Orvus detergent, Udder Cream, cow magnets)

Nasco-Modesto
4825 Stoddard Rd.
Modesto, CA 95356-9813
(Orvus detergent, Udder Cream, cow magnets)

Quilts & Other Comforts
B 2500
Louisiana, MO 63353-7500
(800) 881-6624 (Credit card orders), (888) 886-7196 (Fax orders), (800) 418-3326
(Customer service), www.qoc.catalog.com (Mail order)

Redex
P.O. Box 939
Salem, OH 44460
(Udder Cream)

Treadleart
25834-1 Narbonne Ave.
Lomita, CA 90717
(Machine supplies)

Vintage Textiles and Tools
P.O. Box 265
Merion, PA 19066
(Antique tools, tops, quilts, and other collectibles)

BIBLIOGRAPHY

Beyer, Jinny. *Patchwork Patterns*. McLean, VA: EPM Publications, Inc., 1979.

_____. *The Quilter's Album of Blocks and Borders*. McLean, VA: EPM Publications, Inc., 1980.

Brackman, Barbara. *Clues in the Calico: A Guide to Identifying and Dating Antique Quilts*. McLean, VA: EPM Publications, Inc., 1989.

_____. *Encyclopedia of Appliqué: An Illustrated, Numerical Index to Traditional And Modern Patterns*. McLean, VA: EPM Publications, Inc., 1993.

_____. *Encyclopedia of Pieced Quilt Patterns*. Paducah, KY: American Quilter's Society, 1993.

Clark, Ricky. *Quilted Gardens: Floral Quilts of the Nineteenth Century*. Nashville, TN: Rutledge Hill Press, 1994.

Dietrich, Mimi. *Quilts from The Smithsonian: 12 Designs Inspired by the Textile Collection of The National Museum of American History*. Bothell, WA: That Patchwork Place., Inc., 1995.

Herdle, Becky. *Time-Span Quilts: New Quilts from Old Tops*. Paducah, KY: American Quilter's Society, 1994.

Morris, Patricia J. *The Ins and Outs: Perfecting the Quilting Stitch*. Paducah, KY: American Quilter's Society, 1990.

_____. *The Judge's Task: How Award-Winning Quilts Are Selected*. Paducah, KY: American Quilter's Society, 1993.

Muir, Jeannette Tousley. *Precision Patchwork for Scrap Quilts: Anytime, Anywhere...* Paducah, KY: American Quilter's Society, 1995.

Nephew, Sara. *My Mother's Quilts: Designs from the Thirties*. Bothell, WA: That Patchwork Place, Inc., 1988.

Newman, Sharon. *Treasures from Yesteryear, Book One: Making Quilts from Vintage Tops*. Bothell, WA: That Patchwork Place, Inc., 1995.

_____. *Treasures from Yesteryear, Book Two: Replicating Antique Quilts*. Bothell, WA: That Patchwork Place, Inc., 1995.

Pahl, Ellen, Editor. *The Quilters Ultimate Visual Guide*. Emmaus, PA: Rodale Press, Inc., 1997. (Jeannette T. Muir, Contributor)

Soltys, Karen Costello, Editor. *Fast and Fun Machine Quilting*. Emmaus, PA: Rodale Press, Inc., 1997. (Jeannette T. Muir, Contributor)

Stearns & Foster Catalogue of Quilt Pattern Designs and Needle Craft Supplies. Cincinnati, OH: Stearns & Foster, n.d.

Townswick, Jane, Editor. *Easy Machine Quilting*. Emmaus, PA: Rodale Press, Inc., 1996. (Jeannette T. Muir, Contributor)

Waldvogel, Merikay. *Soft Covers For Hard Times: Quiltmaking & The Great Depression*. Nashville, TN: Rutledge Hill Press, 1990.

_____ and Barbara Brackman. *Patchwork Souvenirs of the 1933 World's Fair*. Nashville, TN: Rutledge Hill Press, 1993.

Woodard, Thos., K. and Blanche Greenstein. *Twentieth Century Quilts: 1900-1950*. NY: E.P. Dutton, 1988.

GLOSSARY OF TERMS

ALTERNATING BLOCKS: Set option. Solid, print, or pieced blocks used to separate other patterned blocks.

APPLIQUÉ: A quiltmaking technique. Pieces of fabric are cut out according to the pattern being used and sewn on top of a background fabric.

APPRAISAL: Valuation of a quilt, top, or blocks by a knowledgeable and qualified individual. Can be done for insurance, resale, or general information purposes.

AUDITION: Placing the quilt units on a design wall to determine visual impact. The units can be moved around until, upon a critical viewing, the best possible layout is achieved.

BACKGROUND: Fabric on which appliqué pieces are stitched.

BACKING: Bottom layer of a quilt (lining). It may be solid, pieced, or in another way patterned. Fiber content should be consistent with that of the top.

BASIC: Fundamental techniques of quiltmaking and the least difficult of the projects.

BASTING: That which holds the three layers of the quilt sandwich together on a temporary basis while the quilting is being done. The basting can be done with thread stitching or safety pins.

BATTING: The soft inner layer (filler) of the quilt. Depending on the item being prepared for quilting, and personal preference, the quilt-maker may choose to use a cotton, polyester, blend, or wool batt. Thin batting was most commonly used in old quilts.

BINDING: One method, and perhaps the most common, of finishing the edges of a quilt. The binding can be bias grain, cross grain, or straight of grain. Double-fold binding is generally preferred.

BLANKET STITCH: Embroidery stitch which can be used both for securing appliqué pieces on a background and for decorative purposes. May be an open or closed stitch.

BLENDS: Those fabrics that are a combination of cotton and man-made fibers. Sometimes fabric made entirely of man-made fibers is also referred to as a blend, as is the combination of two or more natural fibers.

BLOCK: A single design unit, usually a square, repeated to make up the quilt top.

BORDER: Outermost element(s) of the constructed quilt top, exclusive of the binding. Generally is thought of as a frame for the piece.

COMFORTER: Thick textile sandwich usually tied, not quilted. May be pieced or plain.

COMPATIBLE (color and fiber content): Elements that coexist and work together to provide harmony to the piece.

CONTEMPORARY: All items which are from one specific period, be that period current or old.

CONTINUOUS-LINE QUILTING

TRACKS: Unbroken lines stitched with minimal starts and stops. Ideally these lines begin and end at the edge of the project.

COPYRIGHT: The exclusive legal right to reproduce, publish, and sell works, be they in fiber or written form.

COTTON: Fabric of good-quality medium-weight natural fiber, preferred for quiltmaking. Should not be too loosely or tightly woven, too heavy or thin, or slippery.

COW MAGNETS: Strong, high-density magnets which can be used to retrieve dropped needles and pins.

CUTTER: An old quilt or top which, instead of being restored, is cut up to make vests, bears, and other boutique items. This practice is deplored by the authors.

DESIGN WALL: Ample vertical surface on which quilt design elements can be attached for previewing/auditioning purposes.

DITCH: Area in a pieced quilt that runs directly along a seam line on the side away from which the seam allowances have been pressed. Also, area in an appliqué quilt which is immediately outside of an appliqué unit.

DOCUMENTATION: Furnishing, or authenticating, a quilt with the use of documents. Can be through historical documents or objective facts.

EDGE FINISHING: Method used to complete the outside edges of the textile sandwich.

EMBELLISHMENTS: Ornaments, found items, etc. applied to the quilt to enhance and complement the design.

EMBROIDERY: Process of forming decorative designs with hand or machine needlework. May also be used for construction purposes.

ENGLISH PIECING: A quiltmaking technique. It involves basting fabric onto paper templates, then, holding the basted units right sides together, they are whip stitched to each other. After sewing is completed the paper templates are removed.

EXPERIENCED: Projects that require a degree of technical skills beyond the basics. Not for the novice quiltmaker.

FOUNDATION: Base fabric used for stabilization when employing certain quiltmaking techniques. When project is completed, foundation is totally covered or removed.

FREEZER PAPER: Used to facilitate both piecing and appliqué techniques.

GRAIN: Refers to the threads of the fabric. Straight grain is parallel to the selvage and has the least amount of give. Cross grain is perpendicular to the selvage and has a small amount of give. True bias is at a 45° angle to the selvage and has the most give.

HAND CREAM: Lotion used to protect and improve the skin while working with fabric, threads, and paper. Should be quickly and thoroughly absorbed. Udder Cream is recommended.

HEIRLOOM: An item of value, intrinsically or sentimentally, that is passed down from generation to generation.

INNOVATIVE: That which is done in a new or different manner. Refers to both aesthetic and technical phases of quiltmaking.

INTERMEDIATE: Skills which are beyond the basics, but are not quite up to those required for experienced projects.

MASTER TEMPLATE: Pattern that is reproduced the necessary number of times for the project.

MEDALLION: Set option. Central portion of a quilt surrounded by multiple blocks and/or borders.

MOTIF: Repeated design element. Can also refer to the design appearing and repeating in the fabric being used.

MUSEUM-QUALITY: A work that is worthy of museum display because of its use of good fabrics, the fine points of construction, the overall good manipulation of color and value, and excellent state of preservation.

MUSLIN: Medium-weight cotton fabric. Can be unbleached (the most common), bleached, or dyed.

NON-PHOSPHATE DETERGENT: Neutral, synthetic detergent that rinses away freely.

ON POINT: Set option. Refers to the orientation of the blocks. Straight of grain runs vertically from point to opposite point.

PAPER FOUNDATION PIECING: A quiltmaking technique. A pattern is reproduced on paper, one for each block or unit needed. The fabrics are then stitched to each other and through the lines on the pattern. After all sewing is completed, the paper pattern is removed.

PATCHWORK: A quiltmaking technique. Can apply to appliqué, but more commonly refers to pieced work.

PICKER: An item (quilt, top, or blocks) purchased with the intention of completely disassembling in order to remake the piece or to use in other renovation projects.

PIECING: A quiltmaking technique. The sewing of one piece of fabric to another to create a large piece of constructed fabric.

PIN-UP WALL: Same as design wall.

PLACEMENT SKETCH: Drawing of the quilt top's planned layout.

POST: Areas (usually square) that fall at the intersections of the sashing.

PRAIRIE POINTS: Decorative edging for a quilt using inserted folded triangles. Also occasionally used on the interior of the top for decorative purposes.

PRECISION PIECING: Accurate method of construction. Templates are used and stitching is done on the marked lines.

PROVENANCE: Covers the origin and source of an item as well as the "road" it has traveled before reaching your hands. This includes dates, names of people, and names of places.

PUBLIC DOMAIN: Refers to items whose property rights are not protected by copyright and whose use is free to everyone.

QUILT: The most commonly used definition is "textile sandwich," a term coined by Patsy and Myron Orlofsky.

QUILTING: A quiltmaking technique. The execution of small, even running stitches which hold together the three layers of the quilt and provide an additional design element to the work.

RECONSTRUCTION: The remaking of an item in order to get rid of as many as possible of its flaws and problems.

RENOVATION: Generally speaking, the restoration of the good shape the item formerly had.

REPAIR: All things that are done to a damaged quilt, top, or blocks to fix the item and make it possible to complete and use it.

REPRODUCTION: An item made to be as close as possible, technically and visually, to the piece you are copying.

REPRODUCTION FABRICS: Fabrics being produced today that replicate fabrics from other time periods.

SAMPLER: A quilt or wall hanging consisting of a variety of quilt blocks, each one different, set together in one top. Samplers are frequently made by quiltmaking students in basic courses. Many teachers find them valuable as teaching and learning tools.

SANDWICH: Refers to the quilt as it is composed of three layers: the top, batting, and backing. The quilt sandwich is held together by quilting, or, in some cases, tying.

SASHING: Set option. Strips of fabrics sewn between, and separating, blocks in a quilt top. Strips may be solid or pieced. Also called lattice or stripping.

SAWTOOTH: Pieced half-square triangles which form a decorative element and often used just inside of a plain outer border.

SEAM ALLOWANCE: That 1/4″ of fabric which lies outside of the sewing line in piecing. It is not stitched down during the precision piecing technique. In appliqué, the seam allowance is turned under the pieces being applied either before beginning the appliqué work or during the process.

SELVAGE: Lengthwise woven edge of the fabric. Should be removed before the fabric is used.

SET: Layout of the quilt top design elements. There are many possible varieties and combinations of sets, such as Sashed, On Point, and Block to Block.

SLEEVE: A tube of fabric which is sewn to the top of the quilt back, and which, with a dowel, lath, or rod inserted, enables the quilt to be hung for display.

STRIPPIE: Set option. Vertical bands of piecing or appliqué alternating with long sashing strips.

TEMPLATE: A firm pattern that is placed on the fabric and around which the cutting/sewing lines are marked and stitched. Generally, light-weight plastic is the most satisfactory material, although cardboard (not corrugated) or other materials can be used.

TESSELLATION: Mosaic-like design using shapes that fit together without leaving a space or overlapping.

TIED QUILTS: Quilts/comforters with three layers which are held together with square knots or bows instead of, or in addition to, quilting stitches.

TOP: Upper layer of the quilt, containing the design elements.

TRADITIONAL: Quilts made using designs which are in the public domain and passed down from generation to generation.

UNIT: Repeated portion of a block. Can also refer to the entire block.

VINTAGE: Those items which are from the same time period.

ZIGZAG: Set option. Uses large setting triangles to separate the pattern blocks.

*I*NDEX